AF609465

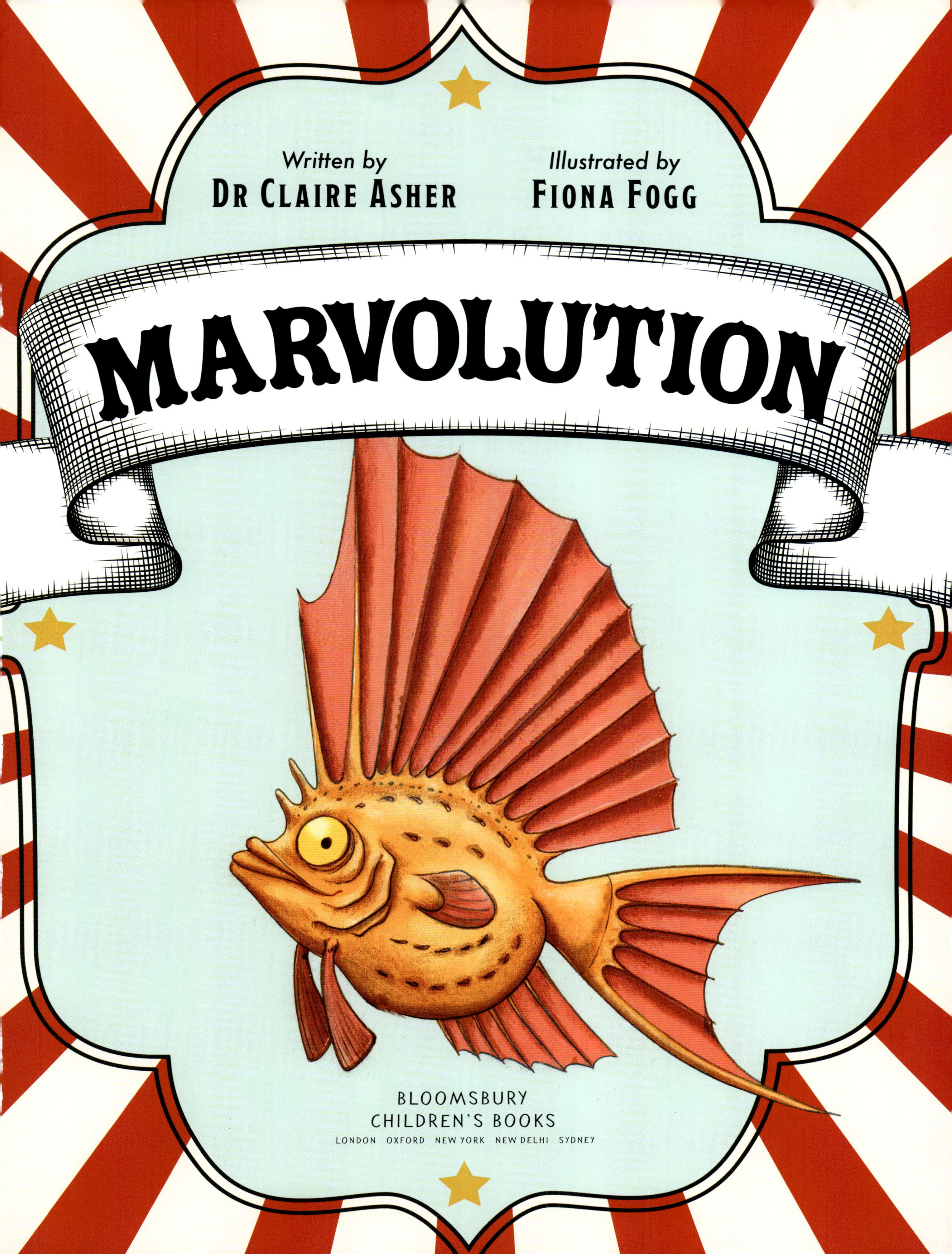

Written by
DR CLAIRE ASHER

Illustrated by
FIONA FOGG

MARVOLUTION

BLOOMSBURY
CHILDREN'S BOOKS
LONDON OXFORD NEW YORK NEW DELHI SYDNEY

For Ted, Rose and Robyn. Never stop being curious! – C.A.

For all the teachers and tutors who have ever inspired and encouraged me, and for all those who inspire the children of today. – F.F.

BLOOMSBURY CHILDREN'S BOOKS
Bloomsbury Publishing Plc
50 Bedford Square, London, WC1B 3DP, UK
Bloomsbury Publishing Ireland Limited
29 Earlsfort Terrace, Dublin 2, Ireland D02 AY28

First published in Great Britain 2026 by Bloomsbury Publishing Plc

A catalogue record for this book is available from the British Library

ISBN HB: 978-1-5266-7126-4; eBook: 978-1-5266-7416-6; Audio: 978-1-0372-0838-6

2 4 6 8 10 9 7 5 3 1

Printed and bound in China by RR Donnelley Asia Printing Solutions Limited Company

Written by
DR CLAIRE ASHER

Illustrated by
FIONA FOGG

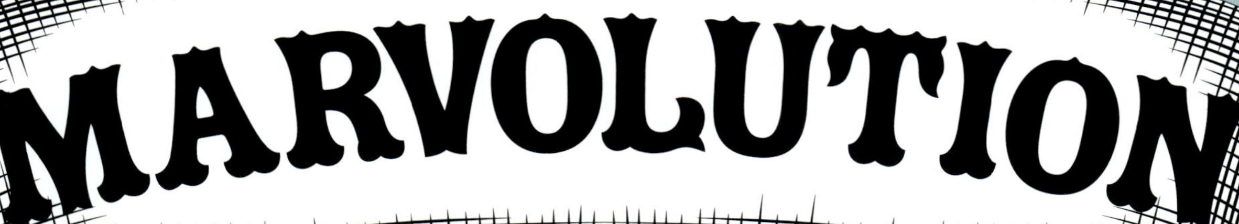

MARVOLUTION

A guide to the EVOLUTIONARY MARVELS of the future

BLOOMSBURY
CHILDREN'S BOOKS
LONDON OXFORD NEW YORK NEW DELHI SYDNEY

CONTENTS

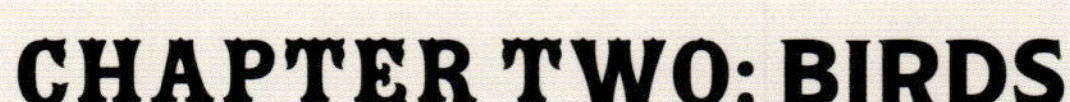

CHAPTER FOUR: MAMMALS

CHAPTER FIVE: FISH

Note on family trees

At the beginning of each chapter, I have included a family tree which shows how the animals of the future came to exist. I hope that this helps you develop a deeper understanding of how these animals came to be and realise that they are not so different from the animals of today, which I refer to in the book as 'modern-day' animals. These incredible creatures are not to be feared or mocked, but rather marvelled at for their incredible evolutionary feats!

Dear Reader,

It is with immense caution that I write this book, for what I have discovered is not something I share lightly. But, as a scientist, it is my duty to report my findings to the world – however strange and unsettling they might be – so that we can all learn more about the wonders that exist within it.

What you are about to read is the result of many years of hard work and planning. I have finally mastered the skills of 'Time Walking' – the art of harnessing the past and future to travel through time. I wasn't sure I would ever make it work, but once I did, what I experienced was further from anything I could ever have imagined.

My first trip to the future was a bizarre experience that threw me into an unknown cavern of confusion, spitting me out millions of years from now. I cautiously opened my eyes and peered at this new land I found myself in. I was surrounded by weird and wonderful creatures I had never seen before. The sounds, the smells ... this place was familiar, yet at the same time, completely new. My mission to travel into the future had worked! But where, and when, was I?

I don't know what caused the extinction of the human race, but humans were nowhere to be found in this strange and fantastic world. However, there was plenty of evidence that they had once been here: decaying buildings, rusted machines and most of all – waste. Rubbish piled high and buried deep underground.

I spent many years exploring this future world, documenting the creatures that call it home. Then, I returned to the modern day to write this book and tell you all about the amazing species I had discovered.

In 1859, Charles Darwin published his revolutionary book, *On the Origin of Species*, which explained how all the different forms of life had come to be, through a process he called 'natural selection'. Natural selection shapes the species that live on the Earth, by favouring the individuals that are best suited to the environment around them. You'll surely have noticed that different individuals of the same species have slightly different characteristics. Some are short, some are tall, some have black fur and some have brown. This variation is fuel for natural selection. In each generation, individuals with characteristics that help them survive and reproduce get to pass those characteristics on to the next generation. And so, slowly, the creatures we see around us change and adapt to their local conditions. This is 'evolution'.

Domestic dog

What I discovered in the future was the product of millions of years of evolution by natural selection, acting in conditions different to those that we see today. In the future, the climate is warmer, the oceans are deeper and the deserts are larger. These changes, along with the relics we humans had left behind, shaped the species that survived and populated the world.

It is my hope that, by learning about the amazing animals that I discovered on my life-changing journey to the future, we can better understand the natural world around us and appreciate our own place within it. Perhaps we can even learn to forge a different path forwards, so that our own species and many others can extend their legacy further into the future.

Sincerely,

Beatrice Russel

Professor Beatrice Russel
Time Walker

CHAPTER ONE
INVERTEBRATES

Invertebrates are a diverse collection of creatures that are ectothermic (cold-blooded) and have no spine. The group includes insects like bees, which have six legs and a hard outer shell called an exoskeleton; crustaceans like crabs, which have an exoskeleton and many legs; and molluscs such as snails, which have a soft muscular body and a rasping, scraping tongue.

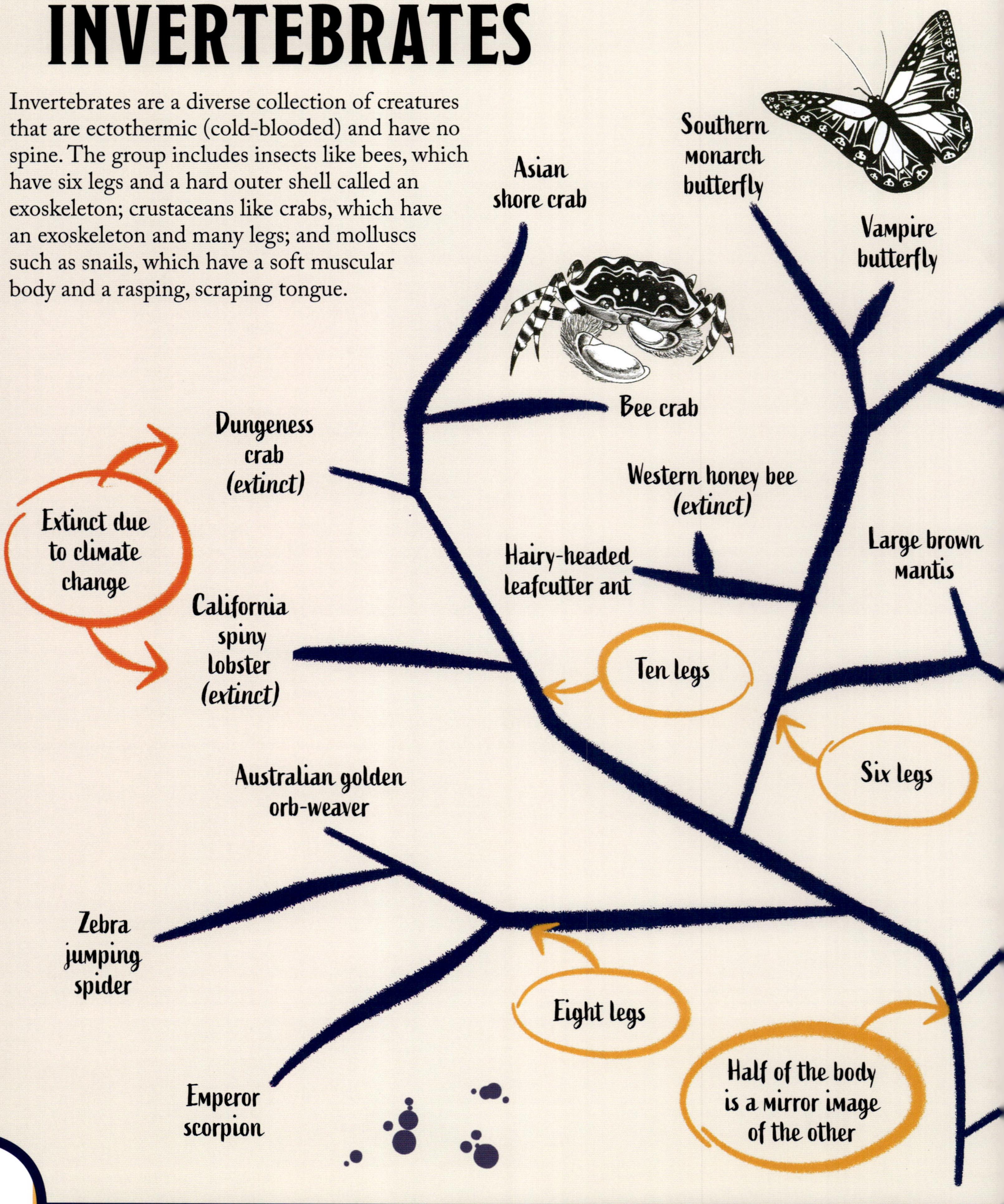

Southern monarch butterfly

Asian shore crab

Vampire butterfly

Bee crab

Dungeness crab (*extinct*)

Extinct due to climate change

Western honey bee (*extinct*)

Hairy-headed leafcutter ant

Large brown mantis

California spiny lobster (*extinct*)

Ten legs

Six legs

Australian golden orb-weaver

Zebra jumping spider

Eight legs

Half of the body is a mirror image of the other

Emperor scorpion

The theory

All living things on Earth are the descendants of an ancient life form that lived many millions of years ago. So, we can think of each species as a branch on the 'tree of life', whose trunk stretches back to the very first life on Earth. It's a bit like a family tree, except instead of individual people, each branch is a whole species. Scientists sometimes draw out these evolutionary trees to make it easier to understand how different species are related to each other.

Seven-spot ladybird (extinct)

Hairy reef beetle

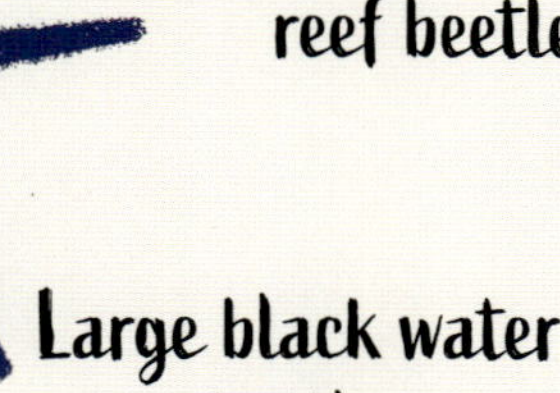

Large black water beetle

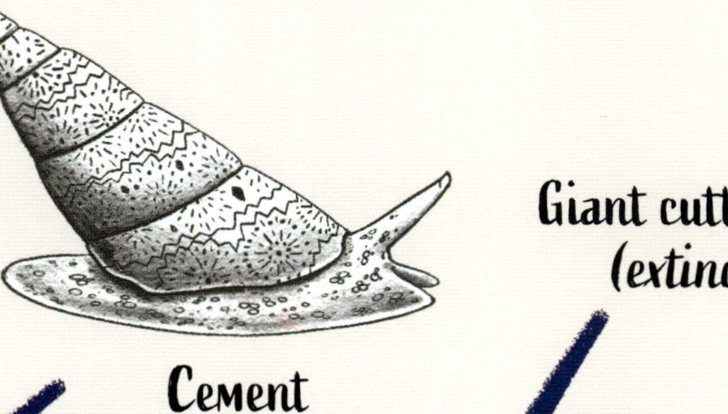

Moroccan bullia

Cement snail

Giant cuttlefish (extinct)

Hawaiian bobtail squid

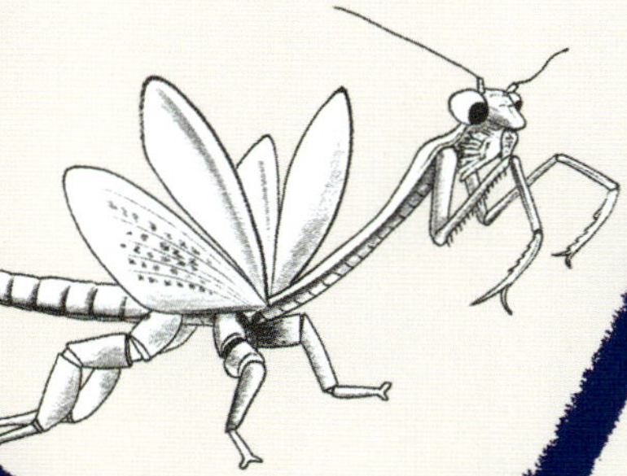

Mega mantis

Leopard slug

Common octopus

Arms and/or tentacles

Black coral

Giant green anemone

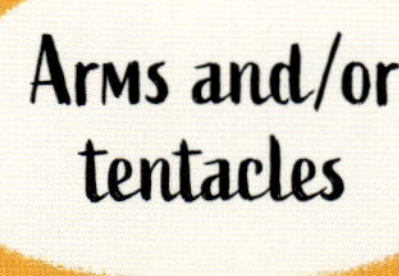

Soft, muscular body

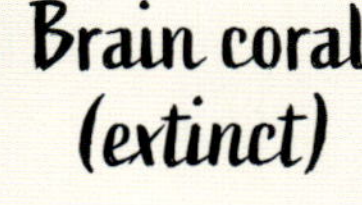

Brain coral (extinct)

Purple-striped jellyfish

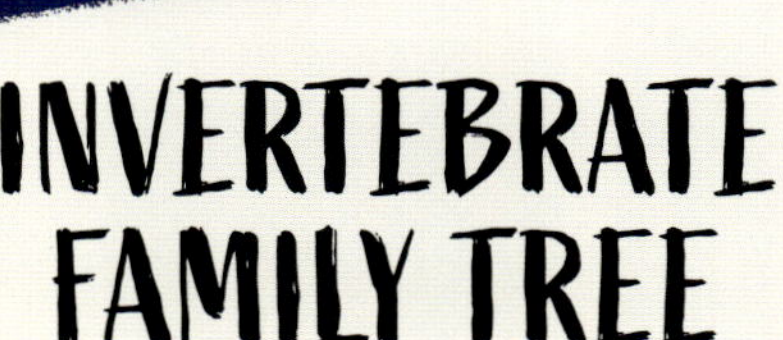

INVERTEBRATE FAMILY TREE

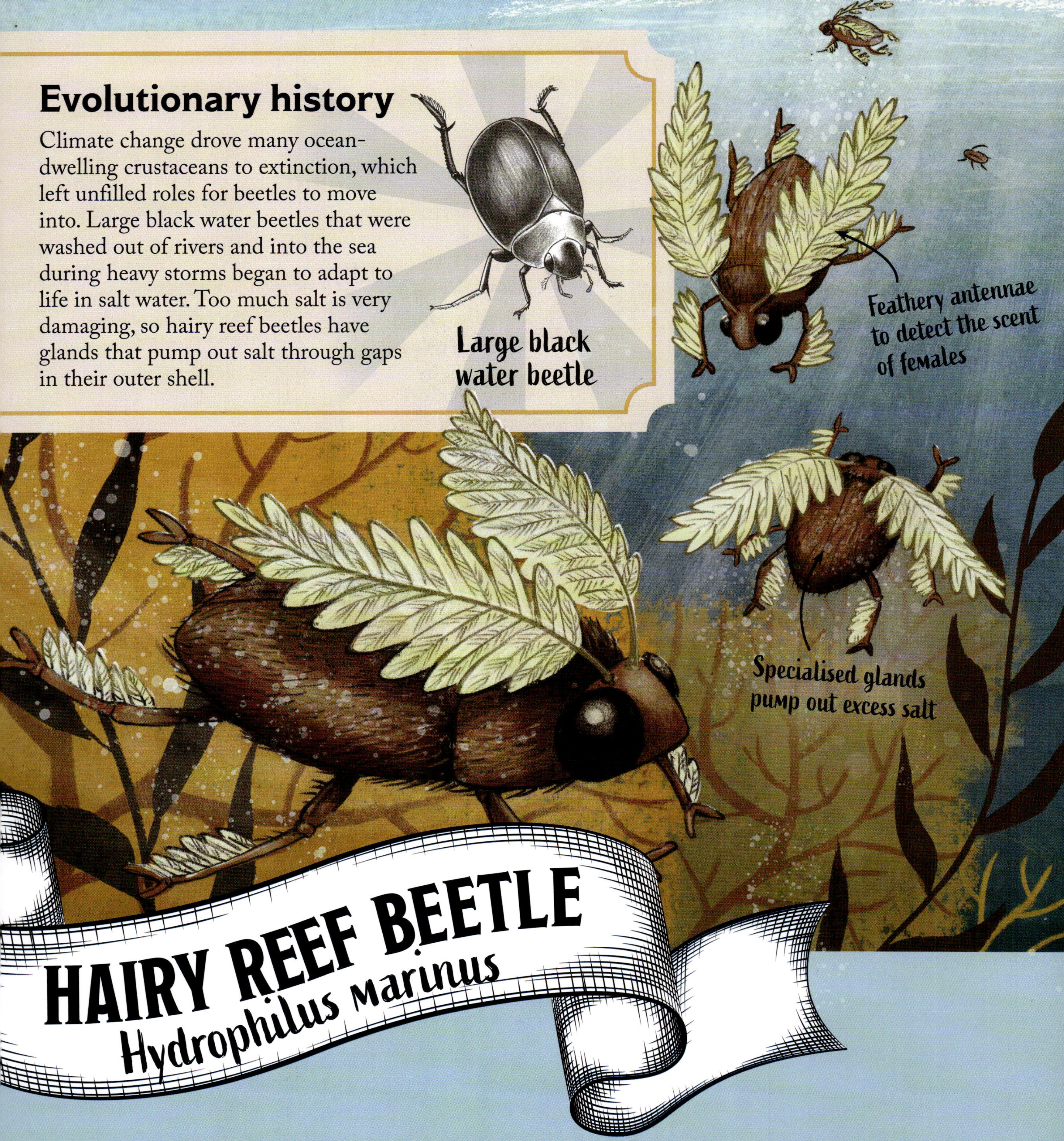

Evolutionary history

Climate change drove many ocean-dwelling crustaceans to extinction, which left unfilled roles for beetles to move into. Large black water beetles that were washed out of rivers and into the sea during heavy storms began to adapt to life in salt water. Too much salt is very damaging, so hairy reef beetles have glands that pump out salt through gaps in their outer shell.

HAIRY REEF BEETLE

Hydrophilus marinus

Small and brown with feathery tufts on their antennae, hairy reef beetles are the only beetles that live in the ocean. They are covered in fine hairs, which trap bubbles of air around their body, so that they can breathe underwater. Every few hours, they return to the surface to trap more air. Females lay their eggs on delicate black coral fronds, and the eggs later hatch into tiny swimming babies called 'larvae'.

Diet

Hairy reef beetle larvae are small but fierce predators, hunting tiny ocean creatures called 'zooplankton'. But as adults, these beetles prefer a diet of plants and algae. This means they play an important cleaning role in their habitat, by preventing the black coral forest from being overrun with algae. Black corals feed by filtering tiny particles of food from the water, so if their filters get clogged with algae, they might die!

Habitat

These cute, charismatic beetles live in the black coral forests that now carpet tropical coastlines around Australia, Indonesia and the Philippines. This habitat replaced modern-day coral reefs that went extinct in the warmer and more acidic oceans caused by climate change. Black corals have an outer shell made of a material called 'chitin', which doesn't dissolve as easily in acidic water and gives them their dark colour.

BEE CRAB
Hemigrapsus pollinis

Small and sociable, bee crabs are often seen scuttling along the beach, their claws oozing with sticky nectar. That's because they have a special relationship with the shorenut palm tree. When the palm is flowering, bee crabs climb up to feed on the sugary nectar. Their hairy forearms get coated in pollen, which they transfer to the flowers of the next palm they visit, pollinating the plant in the process.

Diet

With their long, slender, spoon-shaped front claws, bee crabs scoop up sugary nectar from the flowers of the shorenut palm to eat. They also forage for nuts, seeds and algae, as well as snails and shrimp on the beach or in rock pools.

Habitat

Bee crabs are found along tropical coastlines throughout Asia and Australia. They are most active at night and spend their days resting in the shorenut palm's branches, which they grip on to using spikes on their back legs. They live in groups of up to ten individuals, helping each other to find food and fend off predators, such as herons.

Evolutionary history

As climate change caused the world to grow hotter, palm trees spread across tropical and subtropical coastlines, and new palm species evolved. By then, many pollinating bees had gone extinct, creating an opportunity for the bee crab's ancestor, the Asian shore crab, to take advantage of the shorenut palm's delicious nectar. Over time, the crab's claws became longer and the palms' flowers got larger, helping bee crabs more easily access the nectar and pollen inside.

The theory

When two species interact frequently, each one can influence how the other evolves. This is called 'co-evolution', meaning that both species change so that their features match each other – for better or worse! Co-evolution often happens between predators and their prey, between parasites and their hosts and between plants and their pollinators.

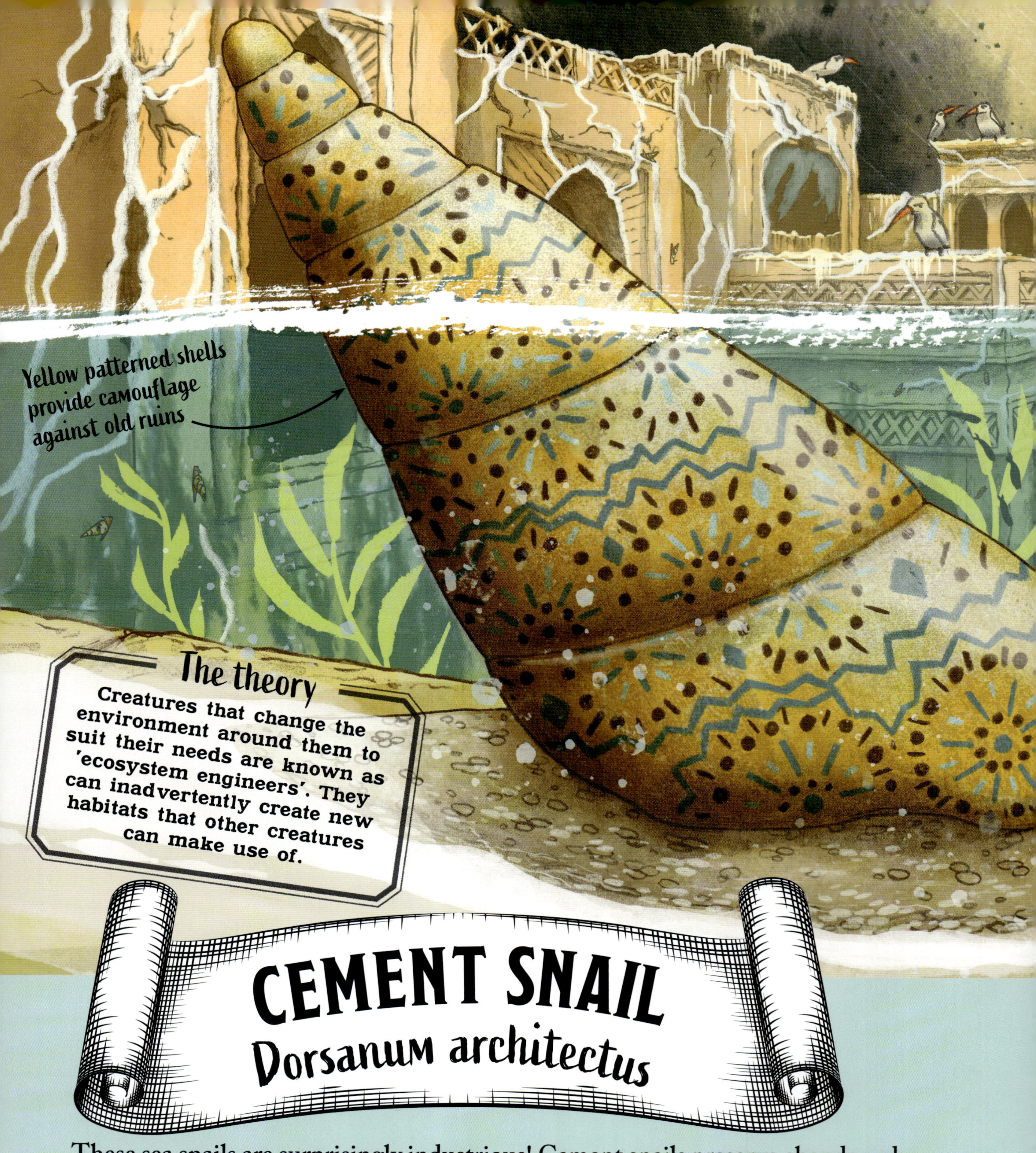

CEMENT SNAIL
Dorsanum architectus

These sea snails are surprisingly industrious! Cement snails preserve abandoned buildings by spreading a thick, slimy chemical that's stronger than cement across the bricks. Several hundred snails live in each building, and together they can apply a coat of slime across the entire surface of the walls every few weeks. Their yellow colour helps them blend in with their surroundings, so they often go unnoticed by hungry predators.

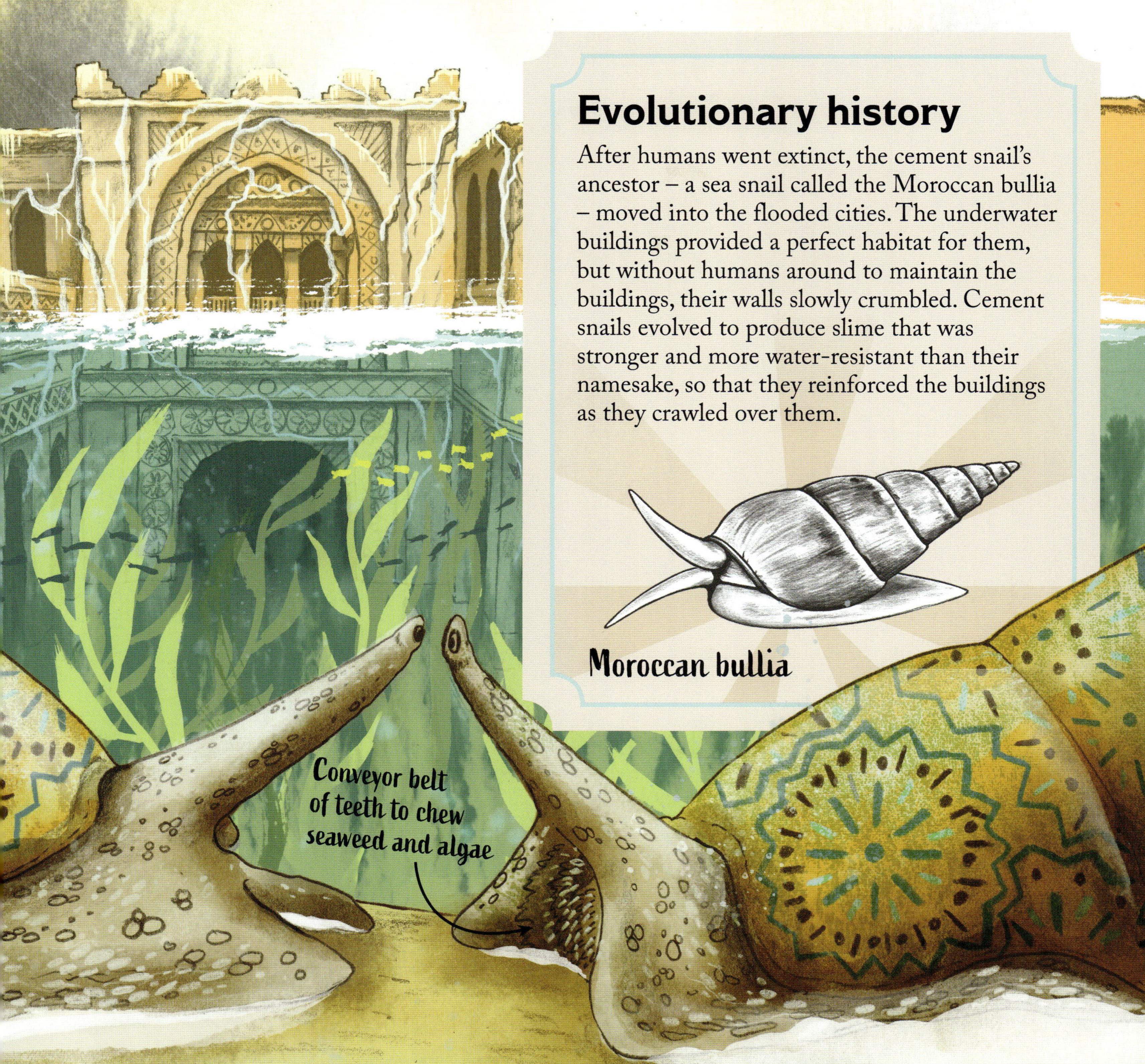

Evolutionary history

After humans went extinct, the cement snail's ancestor – a sea snail called the Moroccan bullia – moved into the flooded cities. The underwater buildings provided a perfect habitat for them, but without humans around to maintain the buildings, their walls slowly crumbled. Cement snails evolved to produce slime that was stronger and more water-resistant than their namesake, so that they reinforced the buildings as they crawled over them.

Diet

Like all snails, cement snails have a conveyor belt of tiny teeth called a 'radula' to chew up their food. They feed on marine algae and seaweeds that grow around flooded buildings. Bird poo from seabirds nesting in the roofs provides fertiliser for the new underwater urban forests where cement snails forage.

Habitat

Cement snails live in underwater buildings in the coastal cities of northern Africa that were flooded by sea-level rise. The abandoned buildings provide shelter from storm surges and tsunamis. Like modern-day beavers, the habitat they've created also provides a home for other creatures. Seabirds nest in the roofs of the buildings they preserve, while fish and crabs find shelter amongst the seaweed growing in these old human constructions.

VAMPIRE BUTTERFLY
Danaus vampyrus

These night-flying butterflies might look beautiful, but they have a dark secret – they're blood-sucking vampires! Feeding on blood gives them a protein-rich diet and helps warm them up, so they can stay active at night and catch their prey off-guard. They have surprisingly long lives compared to other butterflies and moths, living for up to five years.

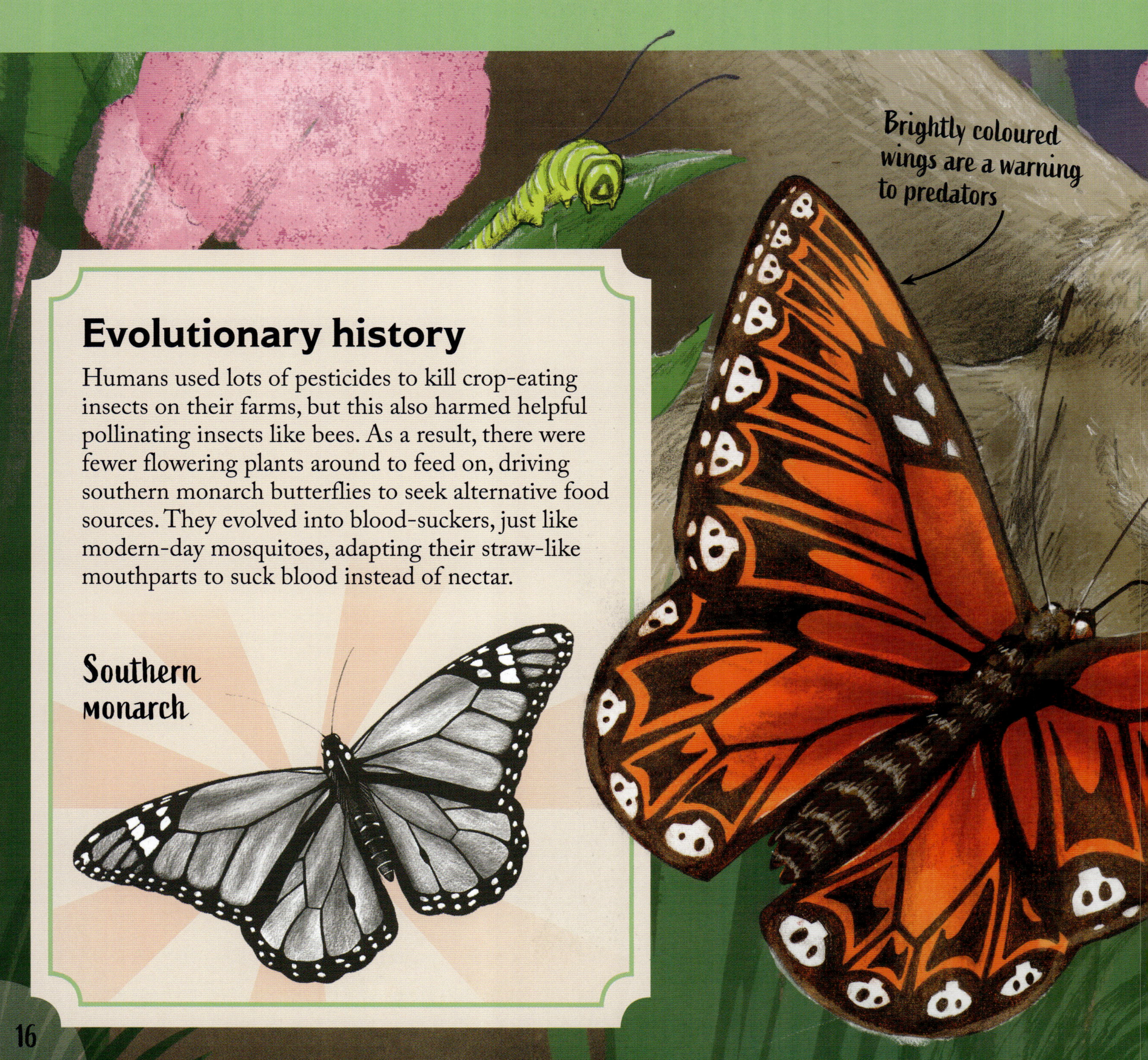

Evolutionary history

Humans used lots of pesticides to kill crop-eating insects on their farms, but this also harmed helpful pollinating insects like bees. As a result, there were fewer flowering plants around to feed on, driving southern monarch butterflies to seek alternative food sources. They evolved into blood-suckers, just like modern-day mosquitoes, adapting their straw-like mouthparts to suck blood instead of nectar.

Southern monarch

Diet

At night, vampire butterflies seek out sleeping animals, landing silently on them and piercing their skin with tube-shaped mouthparts. They will feed on pretty much any mammal, but their favourite meal is deer's blood, and they enthusiastically seek out their musty smell. The butterflies inject a special chemical that prevents the animal's blood from clotting while they feed. They can drink up to twice their body weight in blood in a single meal!

Habitat

Although most common in the former cattle-farming regions of southern Brazil and Argentina – where wild cattle and pigs now roam free – vampire butterflies are found throughout South America. They sleep hanging upside down under leaves, which uses less energy than standing upright. The butterflies lay their eggs on the leaves of milkweed plants, which are their caterpillars' favourite food.

MEGA MANTIS
Archimantis immensa

One of Earth's fiercest future predators is the giant mega mantis. Their long, slender bodies can grow up to one metre in length – making them many times larger than any insect alive today! Their thick, sturdy back legs help them carry all that extra body weight, while their slender front legs allow them to strike their prey with precision. When startled, mega mantises unfold their colourful wings and take flight.

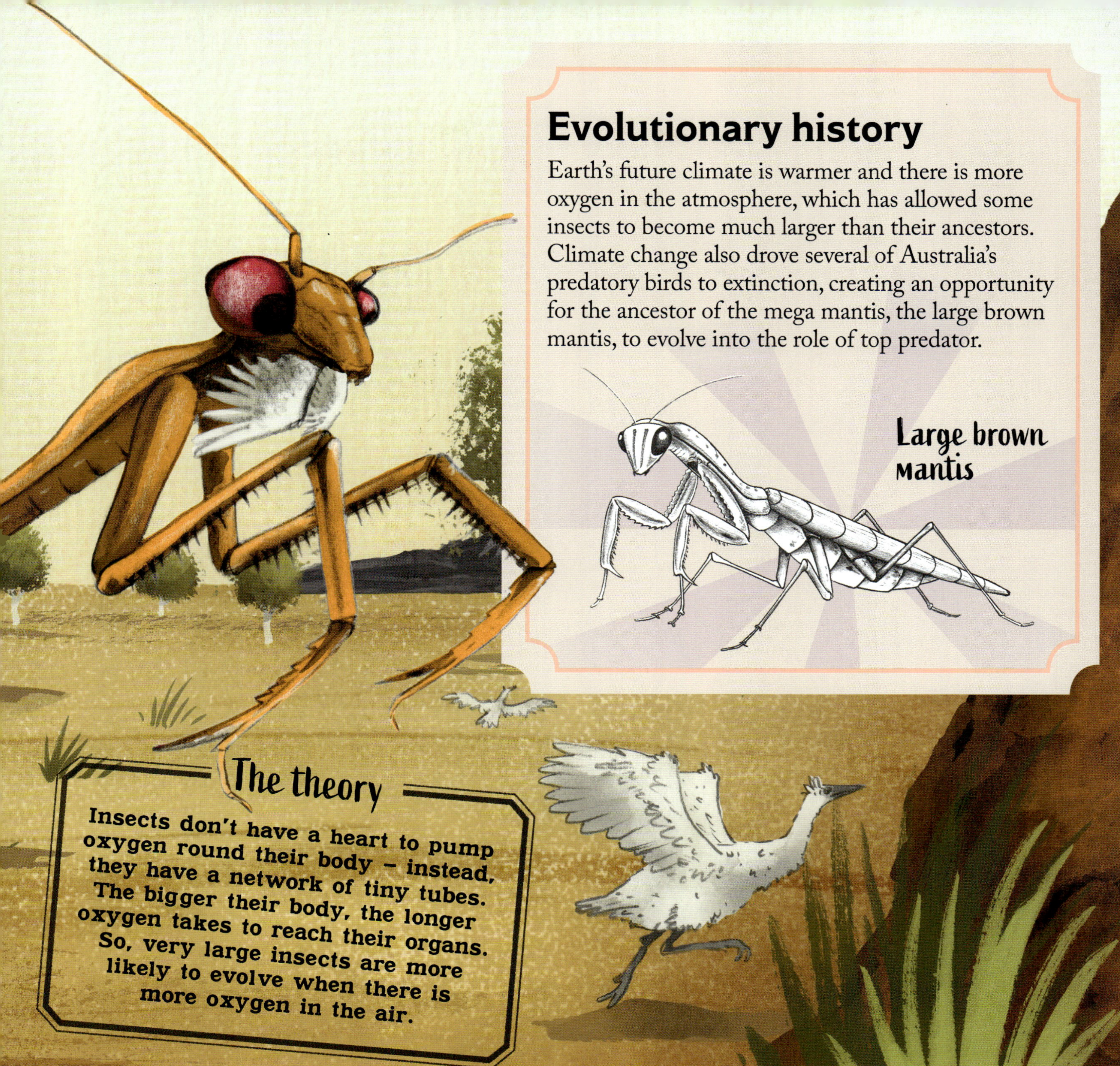

Evolutionary history

Earth's future climate is warmer and there is more oxygen in the atmosphere, which has allowed some insects to become much larger than their ancestors. Climate change also drove several of Australia's predatory birds to extinction, creating an opportunity for the ancestor of the mega mantis, the large brown mantis, to evolve into the role of top predator.

Diet

Mega mantises hunt birds, lizards, possums and even young kangaroos if they get the chance! Their reddish-orange colouration helps them blend in with their dusty surroundings in the Australian outback, making them nearly invisible to their unsuspecting prey, which they devour whole.

Habitat

Found in the grasslands of northern Australia, mega mantises hunt during the day and rest on tree branches at night. To stay cool in this hot, dry environment, they release water from glands at the base of their wings, which cools them as it evaporates. Females lays their eggs on a tree branch, covering them in a foamy casing to stop them drying out.

CHAPTER TWO
BIRDS

Birds are endothermic (warm-blooded) creatures with feathers and a beak, and they lay eggs with a hard shell. They also have a fast metabolism and a strong but lightweight skeleton.

House sparrow (*extinct*)

Ivory cave warbler

Rufous-capped motmot (*extinct*)

Common raven

Feathered flower

European herring gull

Eurasian hoopoe

Eurasian sparrowhawk

Western barn owl

Common ostrich

Birds of prey

Emu

Northern brown kiwi (*extinct*)

Extinct due to introduced predators

Reptile-like jaw

The theory

Natural selection drives species to change over generations by favouring traits that help them survive and reproduce. But how do these small, gradual changes add up to make new species? Scientists have lots of theories but the most common one is when individuals of one species get separated by a barrier, like a mountain or a river. The two separate groups keep evolving, adapting to their local environment, until eventually they are so different that they become two different species.

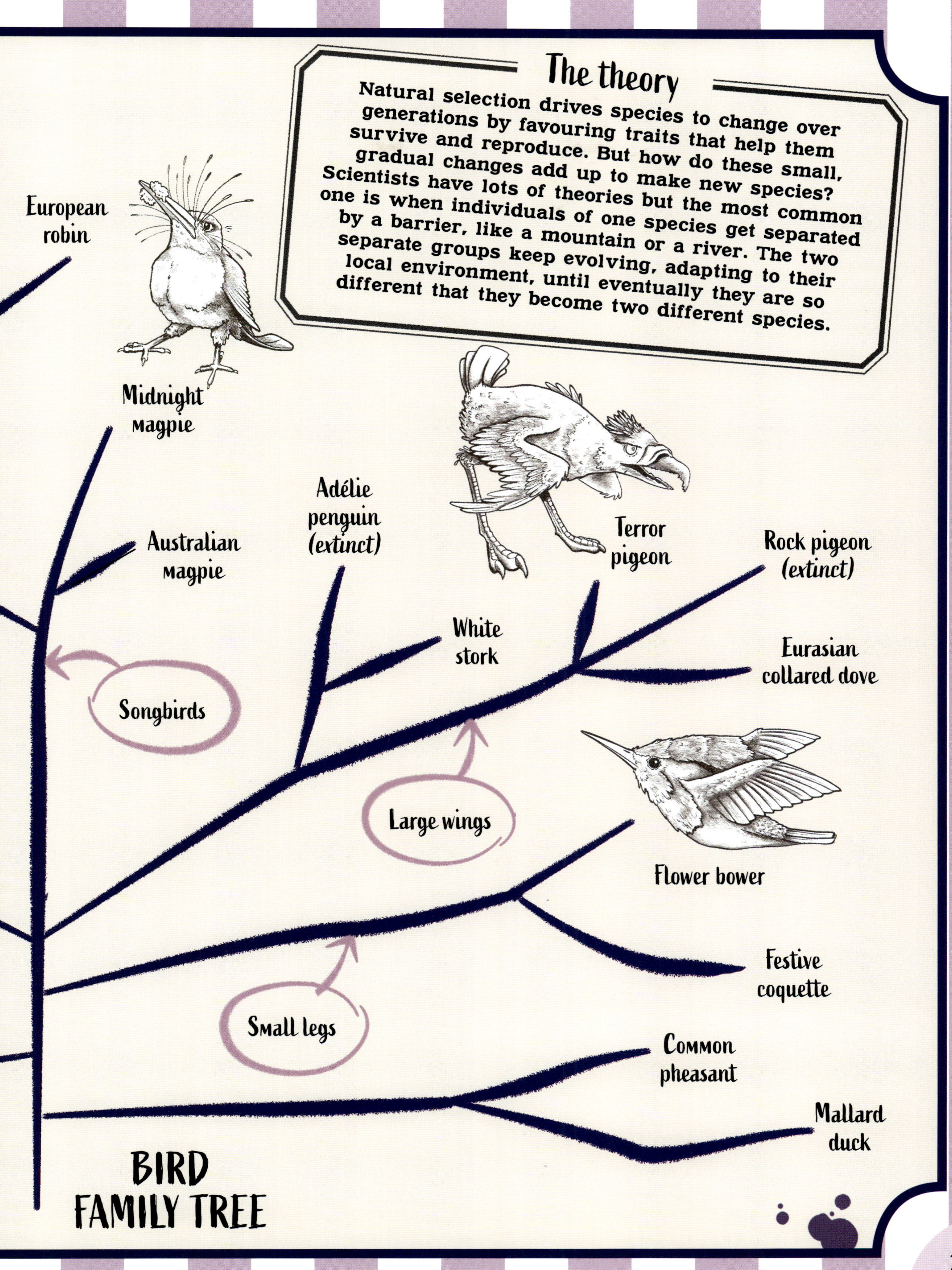

FEATHERED FLOWER
Upupa florida

These flashy birds have a crest of large, colourful feathers around their face, making them look like a flower. This helps them attract their favourite food: pollinating insects. Their yellow beak, surrounded by thin, wispy feathers, looks just like a flower's pollen-producing stamen. When the wind blows, they sway gently, adding to their deceptive flower-like appearance. Otherwise they remain perfectly still – waiting to pounce on unsuspecting prey.

Diet

Feathered flowers are carnivores, feeding on unlucky pollinators that mistake their brightly coloured faces for real flowers. They feed mainly on butterflies and hoverflies. If they get the chance, they will even eat small pollinating birds like hummingbirds!

Habitat

This species is found in grasslands across Europe, Asia and northern Africa. They build their nests under thick bushes or shrubs, to stay safe from potential predators. During the day, they position themselves amongst long grass and flowers, where they can attract their prey.

Evolutionary history

Feathered flowers are descendants of modern-day Eurasian hoopoes – medium-sized insect-eating birds with a crest of feathers on their head. As the climate warmed, grasslands expanded, and the ancestors of feathered flowers took advantage of the abundance of pollinating insects and birds.

MIDNIGHT MAGPIE
Gymnorhina umbra

Midnight magpies are intelligent, nocturnal birds whose melodic songs echo eerily through the night. Their emerald green feathers help them to blend in with the forest floor. Although capable of flight, they prefer to spend their time on the ground, where their food is located. Perhaps with a few more million years of evolution, they might become totally flightless.

Evolutionary history

As daytime temperatures soared in the warmer climate, the descendants of Australian magpies became more active at night. Eventually, they became fully nocturnal. Like modern-day kiwi birds, midnight magpies evolved a heightened sense of hearing and smell, alongside sensitive beak feathers that help them find their way in the dark.

Australian magpie

Diet

These omnivorous birds feed on worms, insects, plant roots and vegetables like potatoes and yams, below ground. At night, they wander the forest, poking their beaks into the soil and leaf litter. Foraging in small groups, they tend to spread out across the forest floor to cover more ground. Their haunting calls help them to stay in contact with one another in the dark.

Habitat

Found in tropical forests across southern Australia, midnight magpies spend their days sleeping in underground burrows to avoid the sweltering temperatures above ground. They also retreat to their burrows to avoid predators like cats and foxes. In the spring, they line their burrow with leaves and lay a single egg.

IVORY CAVE WARBLER

Baryphthengus albus

These ghostly birds are completely blind, and their feathers are colourless. This is because they spend their entire lives in complete darkness. They live below ground in the abandoned mines and tunnels that humans left behind. Without sight, they are very vulnerable above ground, but once a year, in the dead of night, ivory cave warblers leave the safety of their mine to disperse and find a mate.

Diet

Ivory cave warblers feed on the plentiful supply of spiders and insects that have also taken up residence in the abandoned mines. Hunting in total darkness, they rely on their excellent hearing to detect the tiny sounds of insects scuttling about on the mine floor and walls.

Habitat

Found in South America, ivory cave warblers build their nests in small hollows in the mine walls. They collect moss that grows near the mine entrance to provide a soft lining for their nests. Sharp claws on their wings help them to grip the slippery cave walls so they can move around.

The theory

Animals can evolve new characteristics that help them survive or lose existing ones that they no longer need. This is sometimes called 'regressive' or 'reverse' evolution, but it is driven by the same process as regular evolution: natural selection.

Evolutionary history

To escape the scorching temperatures above ground, the descendants of modern-day rufous-capped motmots moved into abandoned mines. These underground habitats offered them protection from above-ground predators, and gave them plenty of insects to eat. Like other creatures that live in total darkness, ivory cave warblers quickly lost their sight, since there is nothing to see in their new underground home.

These vibrant birds have evolved alongside another remarkable discovery – the globe bush. Its spherical flowers provide a safe, warm place for the birds to mate and lay an egg, which they then abandon. The flower acts like an incubator until the young bird hatches and flies away. In return, the birds help pollinate the plant by collecting and spreading its pollen as they move between flowers.

Evolutionary history

Flower bowers are descended from modern-day festive coquettes, a species of hummingbird that pollinate flowers in return for edible nectar. Over millions of years, the ancestors of flower bowers developed an even closer relationship with the globe bush, coming to rely on it not just for food, but also to breed. Their lifestyle is similar to modern-day fig wasps, which lay eggs inside the fruits of fig trees.

Festive coquette

Flowers provide a warm, safe place for eggs to develop

Diet

Flower bowers use their long tongue to lap up nectar from flowers, but they also feed on small fruits, including the globe bush's juicy red berries. When they eat these fruits, they also swallow the tiny seeds inside them. Then, when the birds poo, they spread those seeds far and wide, sprouting a new generation of globe bushes where the birds may one day lay eggs.

Habitat

Found in the tropical rainforests of Chile and Argentina, these small birds are always on the move, searching for globe bushes to mate and lay eggs in. The globe bush flowers provide warmth and protection for their eggs, so they don't need to make nests. Instead, the adults spend the night resting in the branches of the globe bush or other trees.

TERROR PIGEON
Columba terribilis

These enormous, grey flightless birds definitely live up to their name. Standing over two metres tall and weighing up to 120 kilograms, they are like urban ostriches. Their huge size means that as adults they have no major predators, but their chicks are vulnerable to foxes and eagles, so they are fiercely protective parents.

Diet

Terror pigeons are ferocious predators, feeding on a variety of birds and mammals, including chickens, crows and opossums. They use their powerful feet to stun and their sharp beaks to kill their prey. Their long legs and two-toed feet allow them to run up to 60 miles per hour over short distances, helping them to chase down their meal.

Habitat

Found across eastern North America, terror pigeons live in the overgrown cities that humans left behind. They construct huge nests for their gigantic eggs by lining old shopping trolleys with whatever they can find. Female terror pigeons work together to guard each other's eggs and, once they've hatched, to protect the young chicks from predators.

Evolutionary history

In the absence of humans and the scraps of food they dropped, city pigeons had to find a new source of food. Over time, they evolved from unassuming 400 grams creatures into these intimidating 100 kilograms beasts. In the process, they gave up their ability to fly and became formidable ground-based predators.

The theory

Evolution can come up with the same idea more than once. This is known as 'convergent evolution', which means two distantly related species end up looking similar because they faced the same challenges and evolved similar solutions.

CHAPTER THREE
REPTILES AND AMPHIBIANS

Reptiles and amphibians are ectothermic (cold-blooded) creatures with four legs (except snakes, which have no legs). Although often grouped together, they are actually quite different! Amphibians have smooth, wet skin, whereas reptiles have dry, scaly skin. Amphibians lay eggs in water, where they hatch into tiny swimming larvae. Later, the larvae transform into their adult form. In contrast, reptiles lay leathery eggs on land, or give birth to live young, and their young are small versions of the adults.

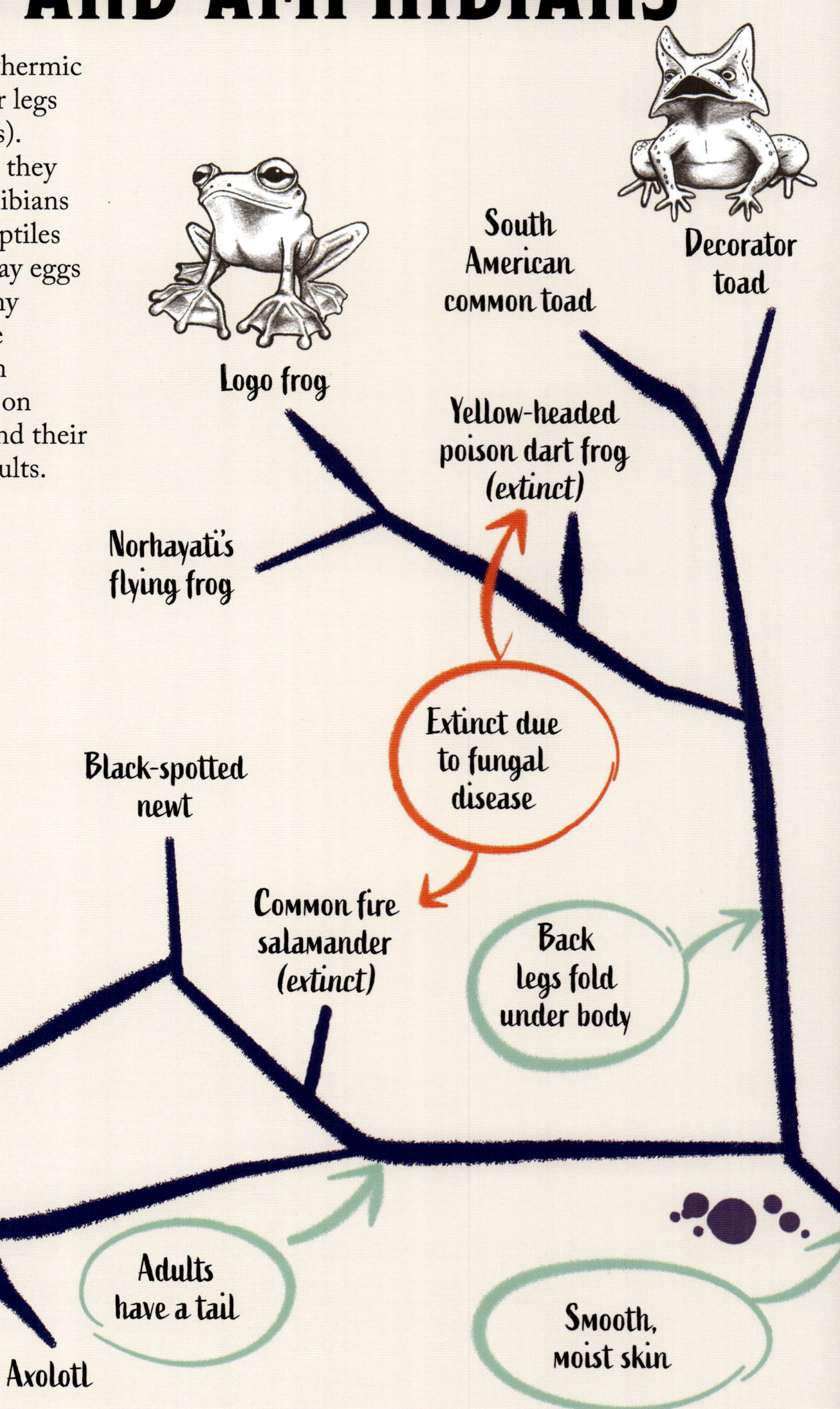

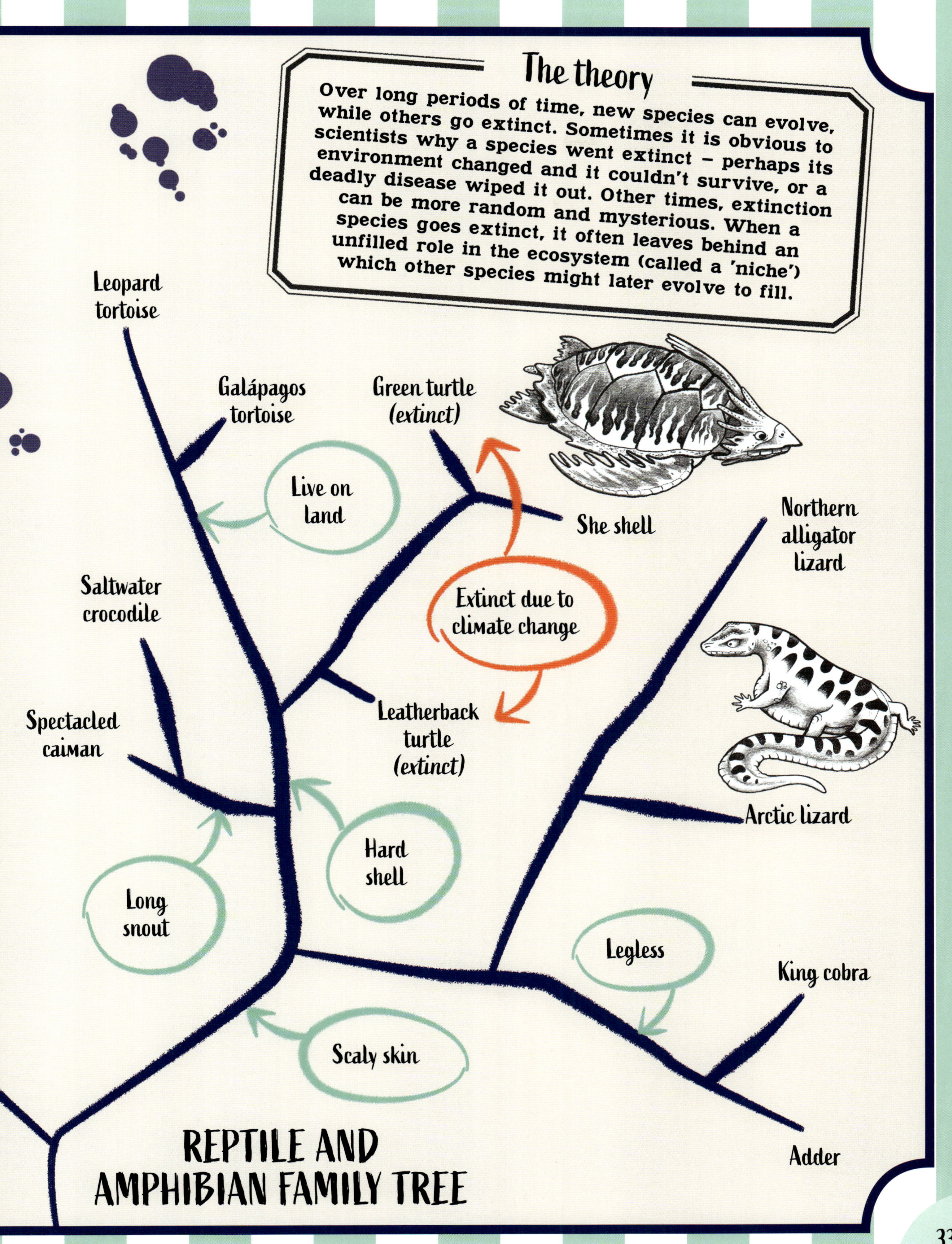
The theory
Over long periods of time, new species can evolve, while others go extinct. Sometimes it is obvious to scientists why a species went extinct – perhaps its environment changed and it couldn't survive, or a deadly disease wiped it out. Other times, extinction can be more random and mysterious. When a species goes extinct, it often leaves behind an unfilled role in the ecosystem (called a 'niche') which other species might later evolve to fill.
Leopard tortoise
Galápagos tortoise
Green turtle (extinct)
Live on land
She shell
Northern alligator lizard
Saltwater crocodile
Extinct due to climate change
Spectacled caiman
Leatherback turtle (extinct)
Arctic lizard
Hard shell
Long snout
Legless
King cobra
Scaly skin
Adder
REPTILE AND AMPHIBIAN FAMILY TREE

SHE SHELL

Chelonia feminina

These graceful giants have a surprising secret – all of them are female! Rather than mating with a male to fertilise their eggs, she shells clone themselves to produce eggs with no father. They clamber onto a beach and use their powerful, paddle-like flippers to dig a large hole in the sand, where they lay their eggs. The spines on their flippers act like a comb, removing stones and other debris from the sand as they dig. They then bury the eggs to protect them and return to the ocean.

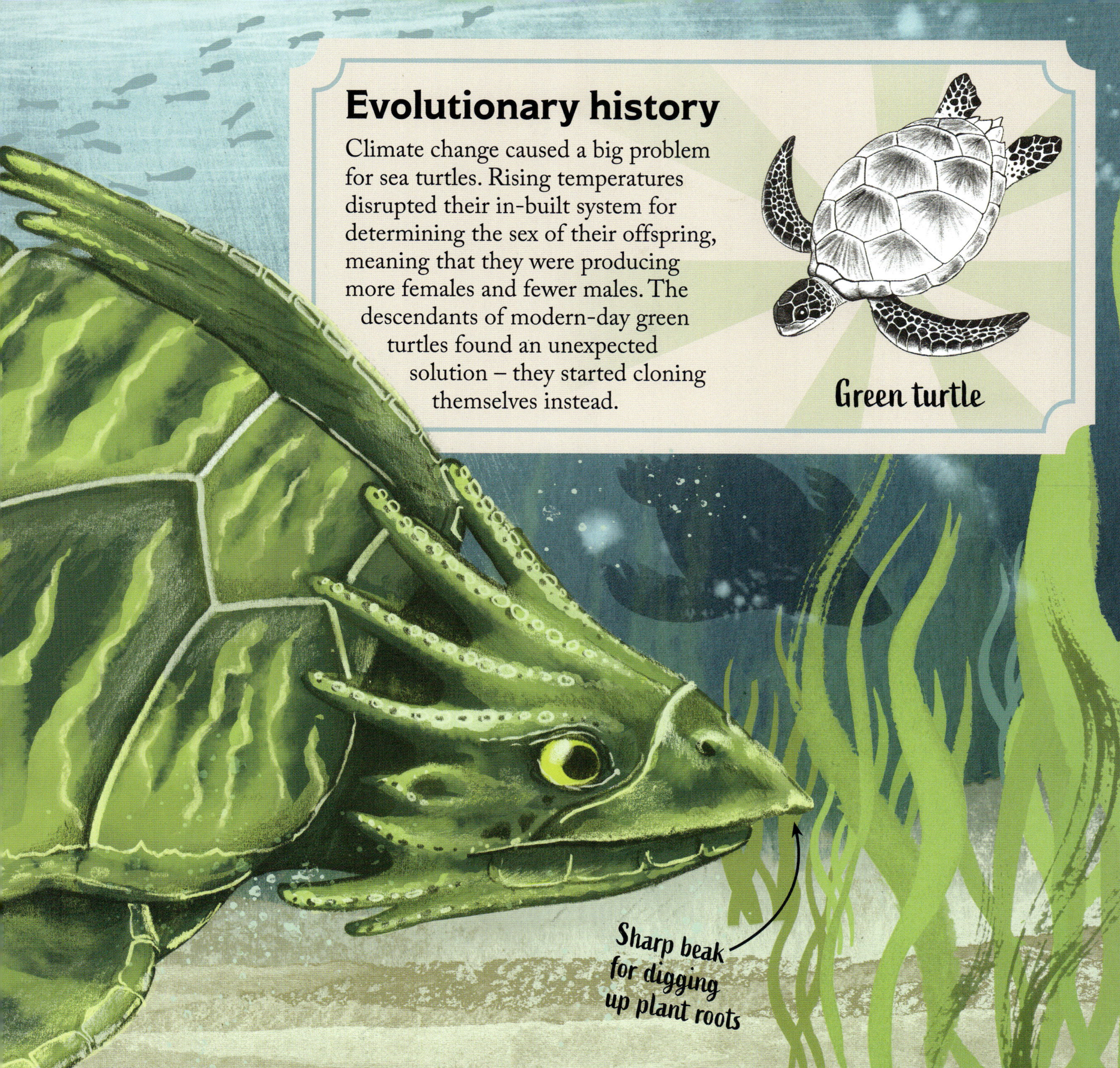

Evolutionary history

Climate change caused a big problem for sea turtles. Rising temperatures disrupted their in-built system for determining the sex of their offspring, meaning that they were producing more females and fewer males. The descendants of modern-day green turtles found an unexpected solution – they started cloning themselves instead.

Diet

Young she shells are omnivores, feeding on whatever they can find in the ocean, from sea slugs and marine worms to jellyfish, sponges and aquatic plants. But adult she shells are strict herbivores, feeding mainly on seagrass and the roots of aquatic plants. Their sharp, pointed beak helps them to dig up these roots from the soft, sandy seafloor.

Habitat

She shells are found in the South Pacific and the Southern Ocean. Young she shells roam the open ocean, returning to the coast as adults to graze in the seagrass meadows. They always return to the beach where they were born to lay their eggs, often travelling long distances from the shallow bays where they spend most of their time.

LOGO FROG
Rhacophorus imitatus

City-dwelling logo frogs have evolved the remarkable ability to completely change the colours and patterns on their skin in the blink of an eye. In the flooded cities where they live, you'll often see them (or not!) sitting on old billboards, or floating on discarded plastic packaging, cleverly mimicking the logo. This helps them to hide from predators, such as birds and snakes. They find it harder to mimic straight lines and sharp corners, so they tend to prefer logos with more rounded designs.

Diet

Adult logo frogs catch flying insects, such as midges, mayflies and mosquitoes, which flourish in their millions in the flooded cities. The frogs' tadpoles swim freely through the newly formed city-rivers and streams, feeding on algae and small plants growing on submerged buildings and cars.

Habitat

Logo frogs have made their home in the flooded, abandoned cities of southern China and Southeast Asia. They spend most of their time climbing across buildings, road signs and other abandoned city structures that peek up from the water. They only come down to the water's edge to lay their foamy frogspawn.

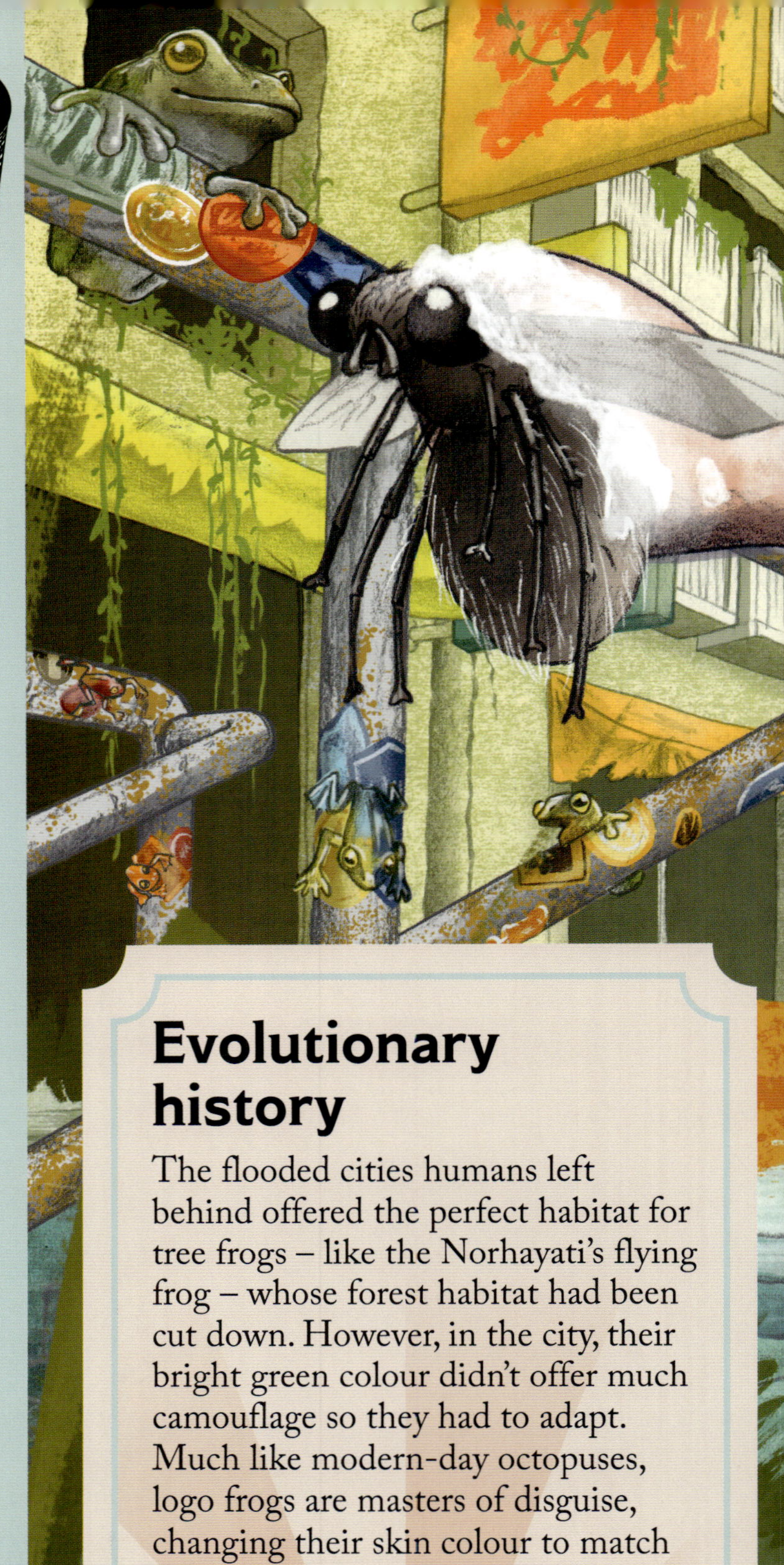

Evolutionary history

The flooded cities humans left behind offered the perfect habitat for tree frogs – like the Norhayati's flying frog – whose forest habitat had been cut down. However, in the city, their bright green colour didn't offer much camouflage so they had to adapt. Much like modern-day octopuses, logo frogs are masters of disguise, changing their skin colour to match whatever they are sitting on.

Norhayati's flying frog

Long, sticky tongue to catch flying insects
Colour-changing skin to mimic discarded packaging
Did you know?
Logo frogs change colour by expanding or contracting tiny colour-filled cells in their skin.

Evolutionary history

Long after humans went extinct, the rubbish they left behind still littered the environment, blowing on the wind and flowing in rivers. The decorator toad's ancestor – the South American common toad – started using this trash to their advantage. Now, these artful amphibians collect only the most beautiful pieces of rubbish and display them to attract a mate.

The theory

Sometimes, animals evolve features or behaviours that make them more attractive to mates, even though they make their lives more difficult! That's because individuals that attract more mates tend to have more babies.

DECORATOR TOAD

Rhinella decora

Despite their drab appearance, decorator toads are the artists of the amphibian world. In the mating season, males collect relics from the human era – plastic, jewellery, electronics, glass – and use them to create beautiful works of art. They display their treasures on the forest floor, and then make a loud call to attract a female. Females are attracted to males with the most impressive artworks and are particularly keen on sparkly objects.

Diet

These large toads eat all kinds of insects, but their favourite food is ants, which they lap up in their hundreds from the forest floor. Decorator toads have special cheek pockets to store pretty objects they've found to carry back to their dens – though sometimes they accidentally swallow some of their stash, resulting in sparkly, multi-coloured poo!

Habitat

Decorator toads are found across South America, from Colombia to Peru, where they live in the forested edges of abandoned towns and cities. Unlike most toads, they are active during the day, when their shiny masterpieces can be easily seen. At night, they sleep in small dens underneath rotting logs or rocks, where they are safe from predators.

ROCK NEWT
Notophthalmus testaceus

As the only amphibians with a shell, rock newts are highly unusual! The thick shell protects these cute, spotted creatures from the jaws of hungry predators, such as birds and fish. It also has a layer of algae growing on the surface, which camouflages them on the lake bottom. If that wasn't enough, the shell also helps to defend the newts against diseases.

Did you know?
Rock newts have specialised cheek glands that produce anti-fungal oils, which they spit onto their shell and then spread around with their feet.

Diet

Adept hunters, rock newts hunt aquatic insects, fish and other amphibians. Their shell's streamlined shape helps them swim quickly through the water when they are hunting. They also feed on a pond plant called contrahongus, which has anti-fungal properties. This is an important part of their diet because it helps them create oils that protect them from fungal diseases.

Habitat

Rock newts are found in lakes across the southern United States and Mexico. At night, they forage amongst the plants in the shallows, while during the day, they sleep under rocks or logs on the shore. If the lake dries up during the long summer drought, they can burrow into the soft mud, leaving only their shell exposed, which keeps their skin moist until the rains come.

Evolutionary history

In the 21st century, a deadly fungal disease nearly wiped out Earth's amphibians. The rock newt's ancestors – black-spotted newts – evolved clever defences to protect themselves, including a thick shell that makes it harder for the fungus to infect their skin.

Black-spotted newt

ARCTIC LIZARD
Elgaria arctica

Well-adapted to life in the Arctic, these small lizards use heat from the Earth's core to stay warm during the dark winter months. They use their heat-sensitive vision to find places where this 'geothermal' heat reaches near the Earth's surface. Here, they dig a burrow, which provides warmth and shelter in the winter, and a safe place for females to give birth in the summer.

Diet

Arctic lizards feed mainly on invertebrates, such as crickets, slugs and beetles. In the summer, they make use of the perpetual daylight to hunt and feast around the clock, building up fat reserves that help them to survive the winter. Even then, they'll sometimes briefly leave the warmth of their burrow to hunt. Their exceptional eyesight helps them to catch prey in total darkness.

Habitat

The evergreen forests of northern Canada are where Arctic lizards call home. Although the polar regions are warmer than modern-day, they are still a challenging place for cold-blooded animals to live. In the winter, the Sun never rises above the horizon, so Arctic lizards have to take advantage of geothermal heat to survive.

Evolutionary history

As the climate warmed, the ice at the poles retreated, paving the way for forests to spread across the Arctic Circle. This created a new habitat for animals to move into. Northern alligator lizards expanded their populations northwards and began to adapt to the extreme seasonal variation in the Arctic.

Northern alligator lizard
The theory
Most reptiles are ectothermic (cold-blooded), meaning they control their body temperature by using their environment. They can bask in the sun to warm up, and move to the shade to cool down. Birds and mammals, on the other hand, are endothermic (warm-blooded), meaning they generate their own body heat from within.
Heat-sensitive vision to find geothermal hotspots

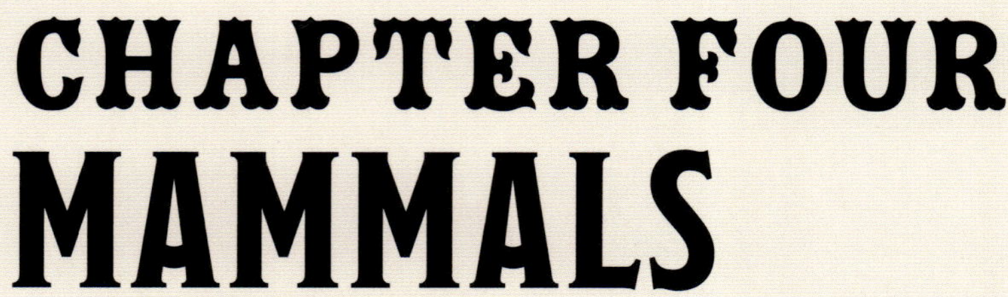

CHAPTER FOUR
MAMMALS

Mammals are creatures that produce their own milk to feed their offspring. They also have fur or hair, and three tiny bones in their middle ear. Almost all mammals are endothermic (warm-blooded).

Desert hound

Domestic dog

Northern raccoon

Sabre-tooth raccoon

Grey-headed flying fox

Domestic cattle

Bunny cow

Hooves

Carnivores

Echolocation

Extinct due to pollution

Common hippopotamus

Sperm whale (extinct)

African manatee (extinct)

Lives in water

Walking whale

African elephant

Bushy-tailed opossum

Eastern grey kangaroo

Young in pouches

Red-necked wallaby (extinct)

The theory

This book is all about the amazing new species that have evolved in the future, but what is a species? You might think that different species always look very different from each other, but this isn't necessarily the case! Even though, at first glance, two creatures look extremely similar, sometimes their behaviour, diet or the way they reproduce can be very different. Only with careful observations can scientists work out that they are, in fact, two separate species.

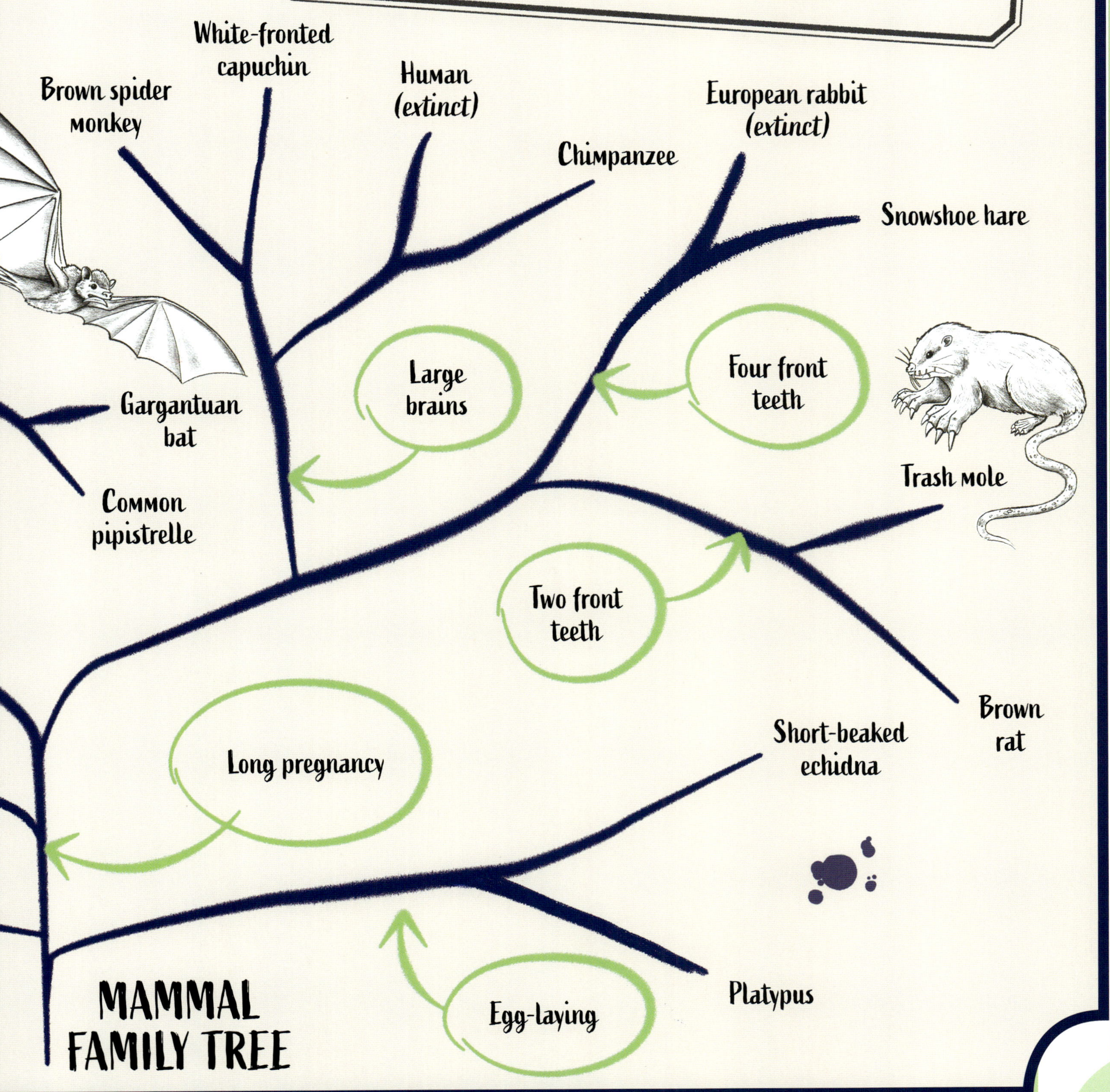

TRASH MOLE

Rattus quisquiliarius

Intelligent and adaptable, trash moles are the kings of the rubbish dump. They have two large, clawed front paws that help them to burrow through piles of rubbish. Their thick grey fur protects their skin from sharp objects and camouflages them against a backdrop of discarded laptops and old refrigerators.

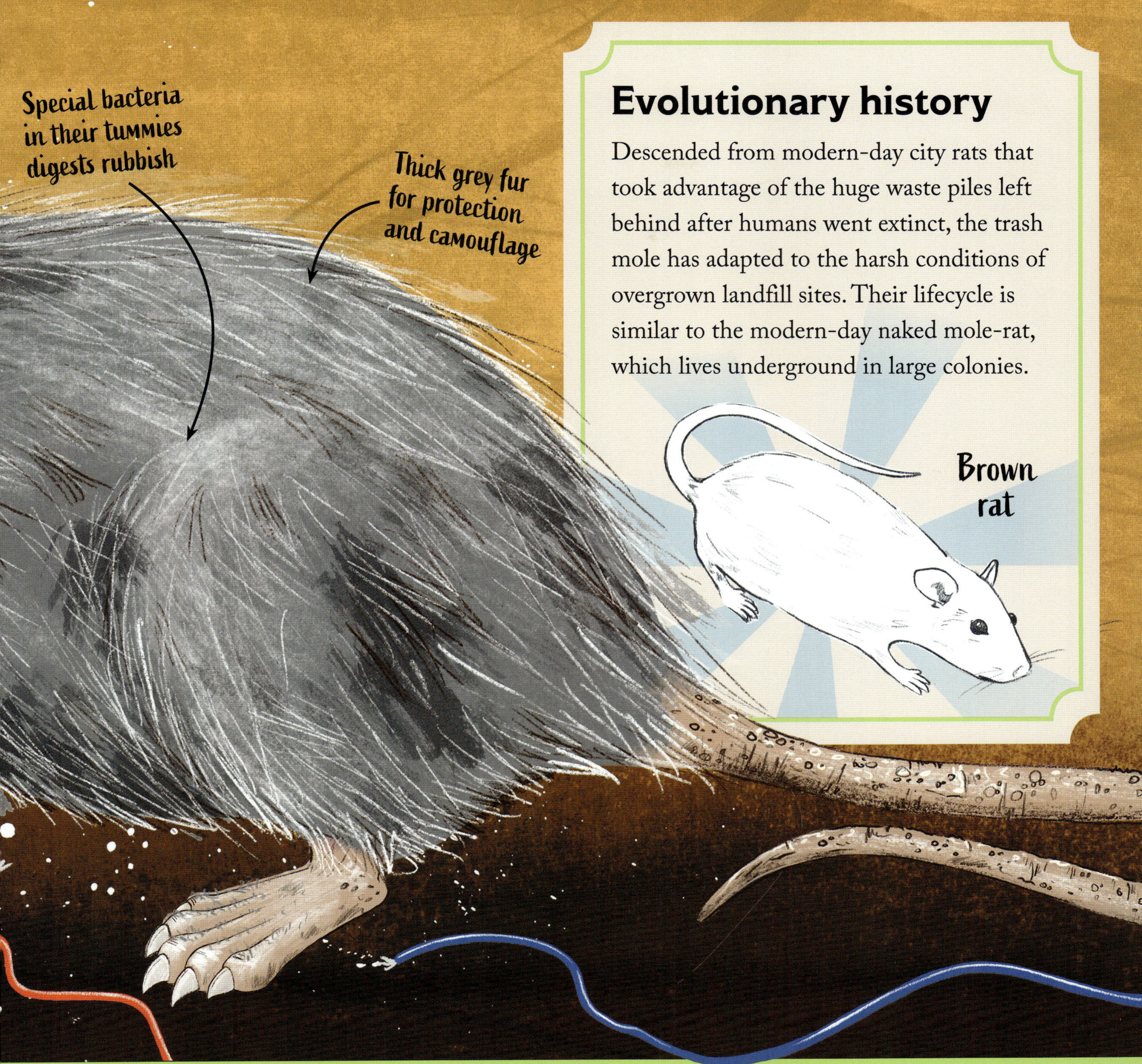

Evolutionary history

Descended from modern-day city rats that took advantage of the huge waste piles left behind after humans went extinct, the trash mole has adapted to the harsh conditions of overgrown landfill sites. Their lifecycle is similar to the modern-day naked mole-rat, which lives underground in large colonies.

Diet

Trash moles are extreme omnivores, chomping their way through all kinds of rubbish. Specialised bacteria in their gut allow them to digest almost anything they come across – plastic, metal, silicon, wood, cotton. This enables them to feed on clothes, furniture, books and even electronic equipment that humans discarded.

Habitat

Found throughout Europe and Asia, trash moles excavate enormous tunnel systems in abandoned rubbish dumps. They live in colonies of up to 50 individuals, headed by a single breeding pair. Pollution has made the environment around the rubbish dump inhospitable, so instead of venturing out, trash moles remain in their birth colony for life.

These small, dog-like creatures are well-suited to desert life. Their small bodies and big ears help them to stay cool. Large flaps of skin on their necks can extend into a pocket, which they use to collect moisture from the air at night. This water also helps them keep cool and provides a refreshing drink, even when there is little water around. Their fur protects them from the sun during the day and keeps them warm at night.

Thick fur to shade them from the sun

Diet

Hunting in packs at dawn and dusk, when the temperature in the desert is just right, these dogs are very adaptable. They will scavenge eggs and the remains of dead animals, and they'll also sometimes hunt desert creatures such as lizards, insects and spiders.

Habitat

Desert hounds are found throughout the vast deserts of the western United States. They dig deep burrows in the sand, which they retreat into to escape the hottest part of the day. Their burrow also provides a safe place to raise their cubs.

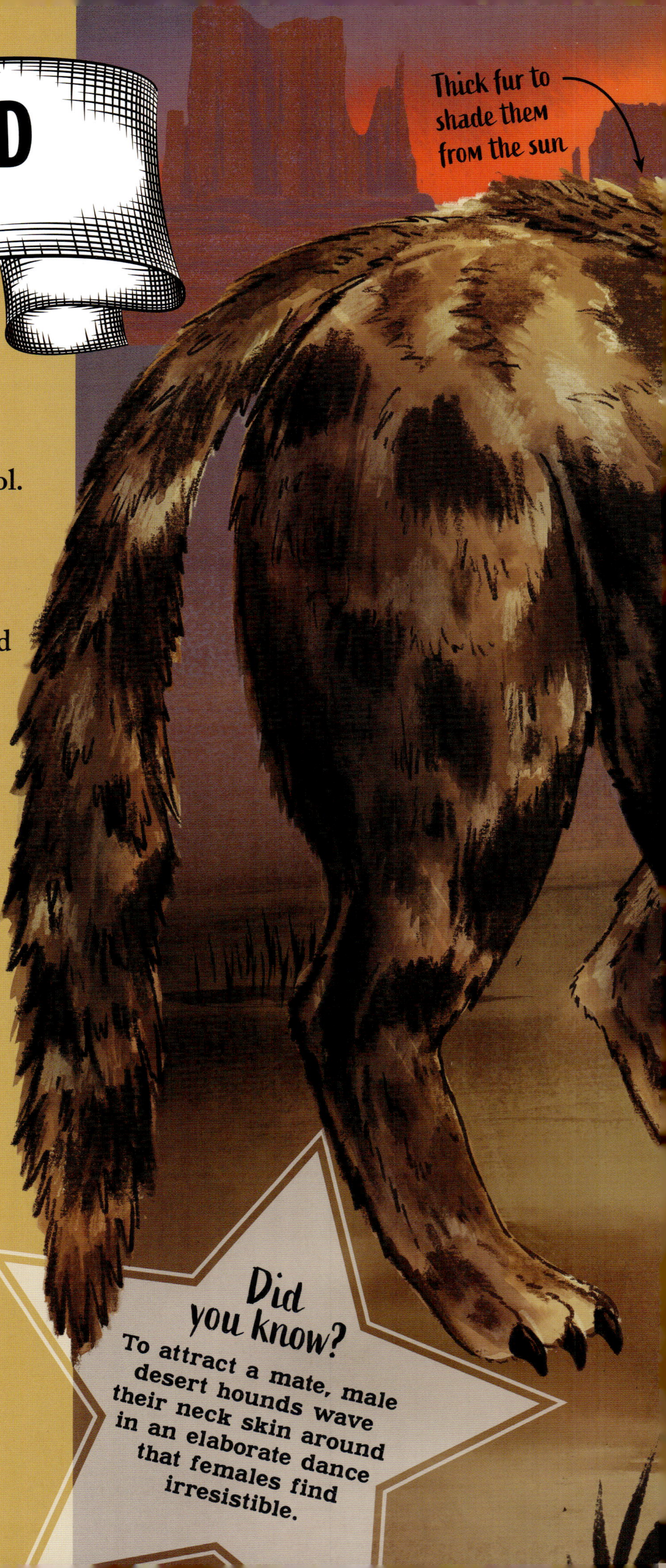

Did you know?
To attract a mate, male desert hounds wave their neck skin around in an elaborate dance that females find irresistible.

Evolutionary history

As the climate warmed, deserts spread across large parts of North America. Pet dogs – which had been roaming free since the extinction of humans – moved into this harsh environment and evolved specialised adaptations to survive there.

BUNNY COW
Bos parvus
These small, hoofed animals roam in large herds across the newly formed island grasslands of South America. At just 30 centimetres tall and with no predators, these adorable creatures are extremely curious and friendly. They are a rich reddish-brown colour, with broad shoulders and stocky legs.
Small body size to survive on small islands
Long eyelashes to protect eyes from dust

Diet

Feeding mostly on grass, bunny cows will also eat leaves or flower petals when they get the chance. This diet is hard to digest, so like modern-day cattle and rabbits, they have special bacteria in their digestive system that allow them to break down all that tough plant matter.

Habitat

Bunny cows are only found on a chain of islands along the coast of Brazil. They occasionally swim across the relatively shallow waters between the islands, but they can't reach the mainland. Their constant grazing stops forests from spreading across the islands.

The theory

Animals on islands often evolve to be much smaller than their mainland relatives. Scientists think this is because resources like food and territory are more limited, so smaller animals are more likely to survive.

Bacteria in their tummies help break down plant matter

Evolutionary history

As the climate warmed, rising seas created new islands. In some places, farm animals like domestic cattle were trapped on these small, grassland sanctuaries, surrounded by sea. As they adapted to their new environment, they became much, much smaller. Bunny cows evolved to fill the role of rabbits in their new island ecosystem: grazing long grasses and returning nutrients to the soil through their poo.

Domestic cattle

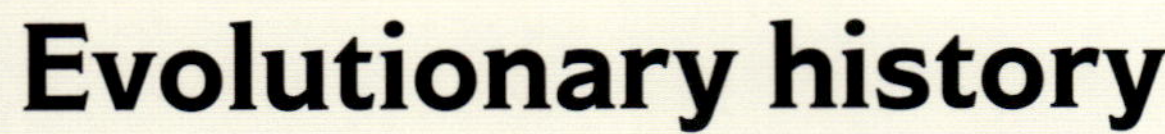

Evolutionary history

Descended from modern-day northern raccoons, these creatures started living in groups to hunt prey as the climate and environment around them began to change. They gradually switched to a diet that contained more meat and, over time, evolved to become social pack hunters.

Northern raccoon

SABRE-TOOTH RACCOON

Procyon fortis

With long canine teeth and sharp claws, sabre-tooth raccoons are fierce predators. These smart, social animals live in packs of five to fifteen individuals. Their huge sabre-like teeth take a while to grow to full length, so young sabre-tooth raccoons stay with their family group for up to two years before leaving to join a new pack and find a mate.

Diet

Sabre-tooth raccoons mainly hunt deer, but will also scavenge for prey that has been killed by other animals. Like prehistoric sabre-tooth cats, they use their giant canines to puncture their prey's skull, killing them quickly. Hunting in packs, they work together to take down animals many times larger than them, sharing their spoils as a group.

Habitat

Found across the southern United States and Central America, sabre-tooth raccoons prefer savannah and sparse woodland habitats, where they can hunt most effectively. They work together in relay to chase their prey across the open habitat until it becomes so tired that it can no longer defend itself.

GARGANTUAN BAT
Pipistrellus colossus

Weighing up to three kilograms and with a three-metre wingspan, these are the largest bats to have ever lived on Earth. Their huge wings help them to travel long distances in search of food, and also keep them cool in the hot climate. They use their excellent eyesight to locate food and mates in the forest.

Diet

Gargantuan bats feed on all kinds of fruit, such as oranges, bananas and grapefruit. After a large meal, they can be so heavy that they're unable to take flight. They simply have to wait it out, sitting on the ground until they've digested their food and pooed. Their ancestors once used echolocation to hunt insects, but their new, fruit-based diet made sight and smell more useful senses for finding food.

Habitat

Found in the new tropical forests of China, these bats live in overgrown fruit plantations that humans left behind. Like many modern-day bats, they sleep during the day, hanging upside down from fruit trees. This means that when they wake up, a tasty meal is usually nearby.

Large wings help them lose body heat to stay cool

Evolutionary history

Humans used large amounts of pesticides on farms and gardens to kill insects. As a result of this, many insect-eating bats went extinct. To survive, the tiny pipistrelle bat started eating fruit, which allowed them to grow much larger because – like many modern-day fruit-eating bats – they no longer relied on echolocation to find food.

Pipistrelle bat

The theory

Echolocation is when small animals create high-pitched sounds that bounce off objects, then listen for the returning echoes to create a picture of their surroundings. Larger animals tend to produce lower-pitched noises, so they can't use this skill.

WALKING WHALE
Physeter ambulans

Fleeing oceans that had been polluted with plastic and turned acidic because of climate change, the ancestors of these whales returned to the land. Their flippers evolved into front feet and their tails became smaller, allowing them to move about outside the water. Adult walking whales are around three metres long – a lot smaller than their ocean cousins, but still a deadly mammal you wouldn't want to encounter!

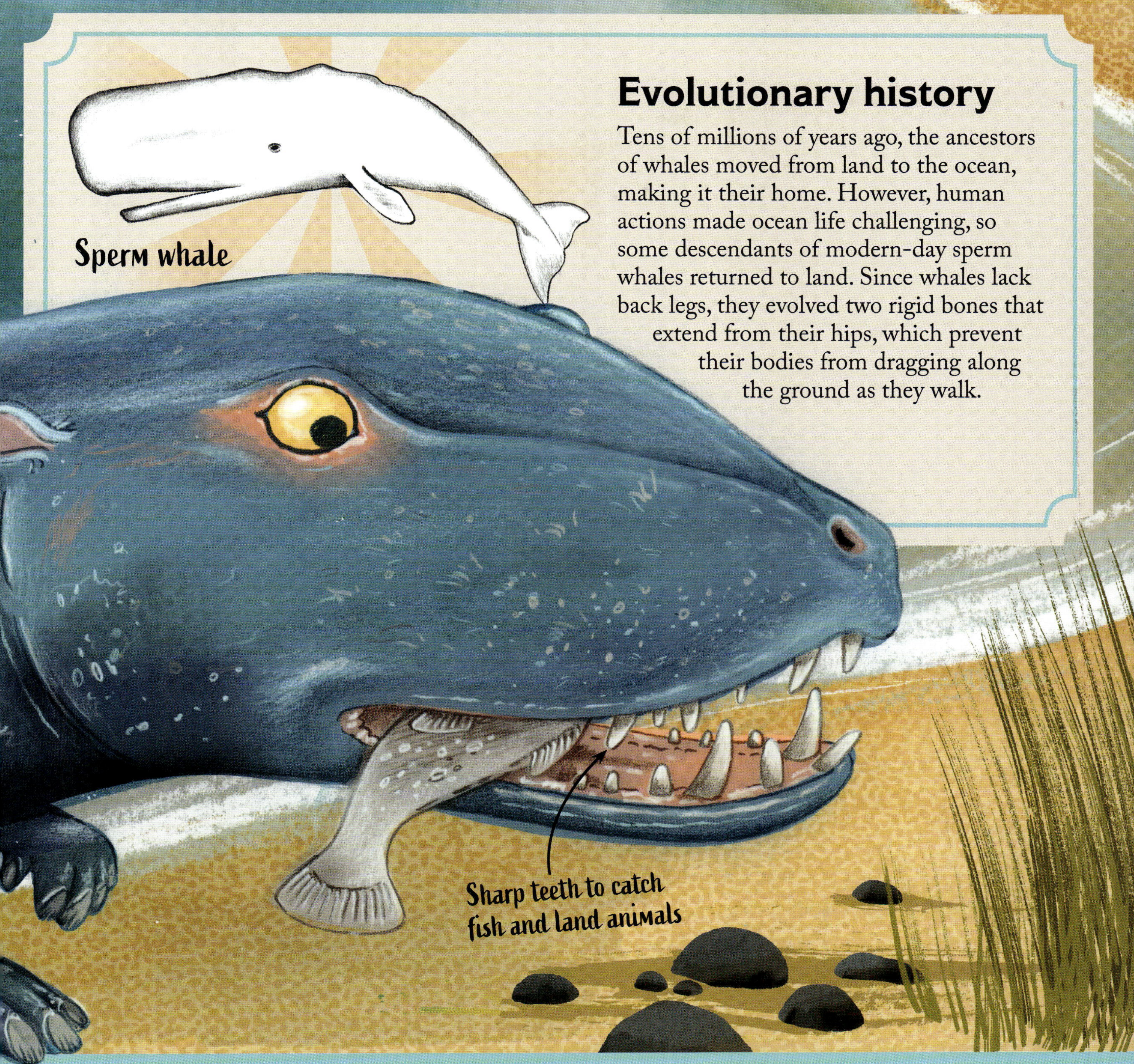

Evolutionary history

Tens of millions of years ago, the ancestors of whales moved from land to the ocean, making it their home. However, human actions made ocean life challenging, so some descendants of modern-day sperm whales returned to land. Since whales lack back legs, they evolved two rigid bones that extend from their hips, which prevent their bodies from dragging along the ground as they walk.

Diet

Walking whales feed on large fish and animals that visit the river to drink, such as rodents and antelope. Like crocodiles, they often sit just below the water, waiting for prey to come close before they pounce. Although they have few predators, walking whales are sometimes attacked by crocodiles or lions.

Habitat

Found around the Zambezi River estuary in Africa, their habitat offers walking whales the best of both worlds – they can find plenty of food in and around the river, and return to land to eat their prey. Like some modern-day whales, they are able to sleep with only half of their brain at a time, so they can keep an eye out for predators while they rest.

CHAPTER FIVE
FISH

Fish are aquatic, egg-laying creatures that breathe underwater using gills. They have no legs, but they have fins for swimming. Most fish are ectothermic (cold-blooded).

Smarty fin

Goldfish

Grass carp

Punk fish

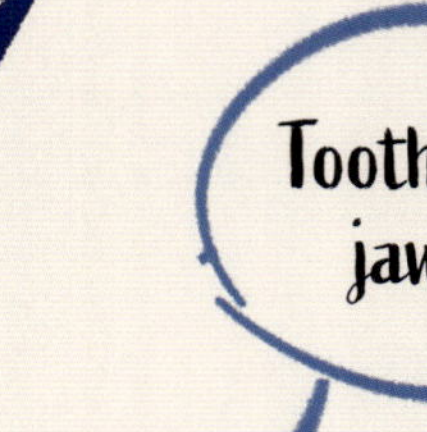

Black piranha

3 fins on back

Humpback anglerfish (extinct)

Gaping death fish

Southern bluefin tuna (extinct)

Thorny seahorse

Extinct due to climate change

Pacific footballfish (extinct)

Fins with bony spines

Swordfish

Spotted moray eel

The theory

Evolutionary progress doesn't always happen at a constant speed. Sometimes, plants and animals stay more or less the same for millions of years. Other times, a big change can drive species to change more quickly. This rapid burst of evolution might be caused by a change to the environment – such as a rise in oxygen levels in the atmosphere – or it could be triggered by a new evolutionary innovation. For example, when a predator evolved sight for the first time, other animals had to adapt quickly to stay alive!

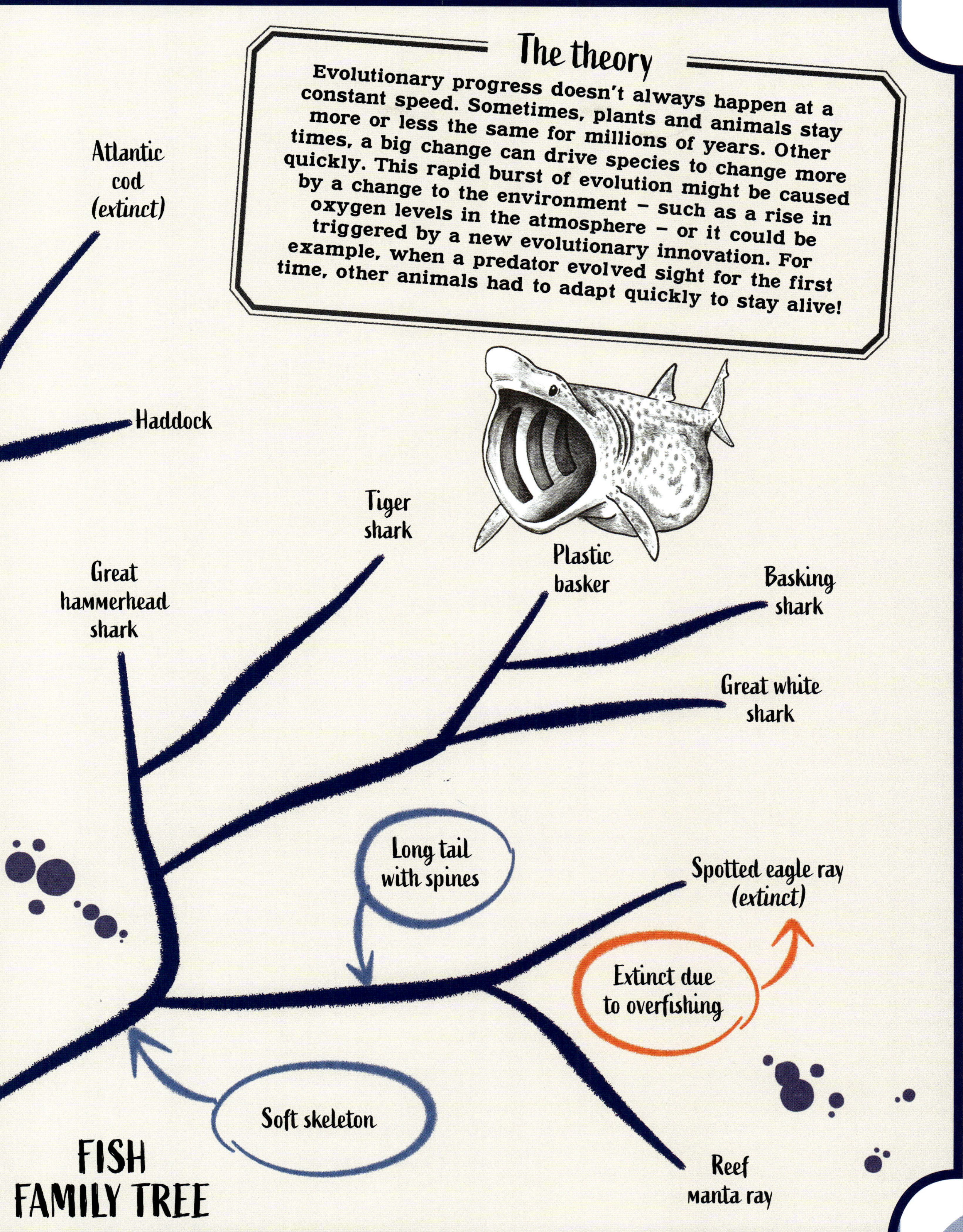

PUNK FISH

Carassius capillus

Chubby and colourful, with a large, mohawk-like fin on their heads, punk fish really stand out. Their rounded body shape means they easily overheat, so they use their fin to keep their body temperature stable. They swim slowly near the surface, sticking their fin out into the air. It's packed full of blood vessels, so this behaviour cools the blood passing through the fin, helping to cool down their whole body.

The theory

Humans transported species all over the world and carelessly released them into new habitats, not realising that they might cause problems. Some of these species attacked local wildlife, competed with them for food or spread diseases, sometimes driving them to extinction. These harmful introduced species are known as 'invasive'.

Diet

Punk fish are herbivores, feeding on lake algae and plants. The algae they eat contains a chemical called 'betacarotene', which gives them their bright orange colour. They have a huge appetite, and often gobble up so much of the food in their habitat that local fish starve. This disrupts the food chain and can sometimes cause the whole lake ecosystem to collapse!

Habitat

Found in lakes across southern Europe, punk fish swim in large shoals. They often stick their heads into the soft sand at the bottom of the lake in search of food. In doing so, they inadvertently disturb the sand, which makes the water murky. This can cause problems for other fish, because it blocks out sunlight and can kill the aquatic plants that they feed on.

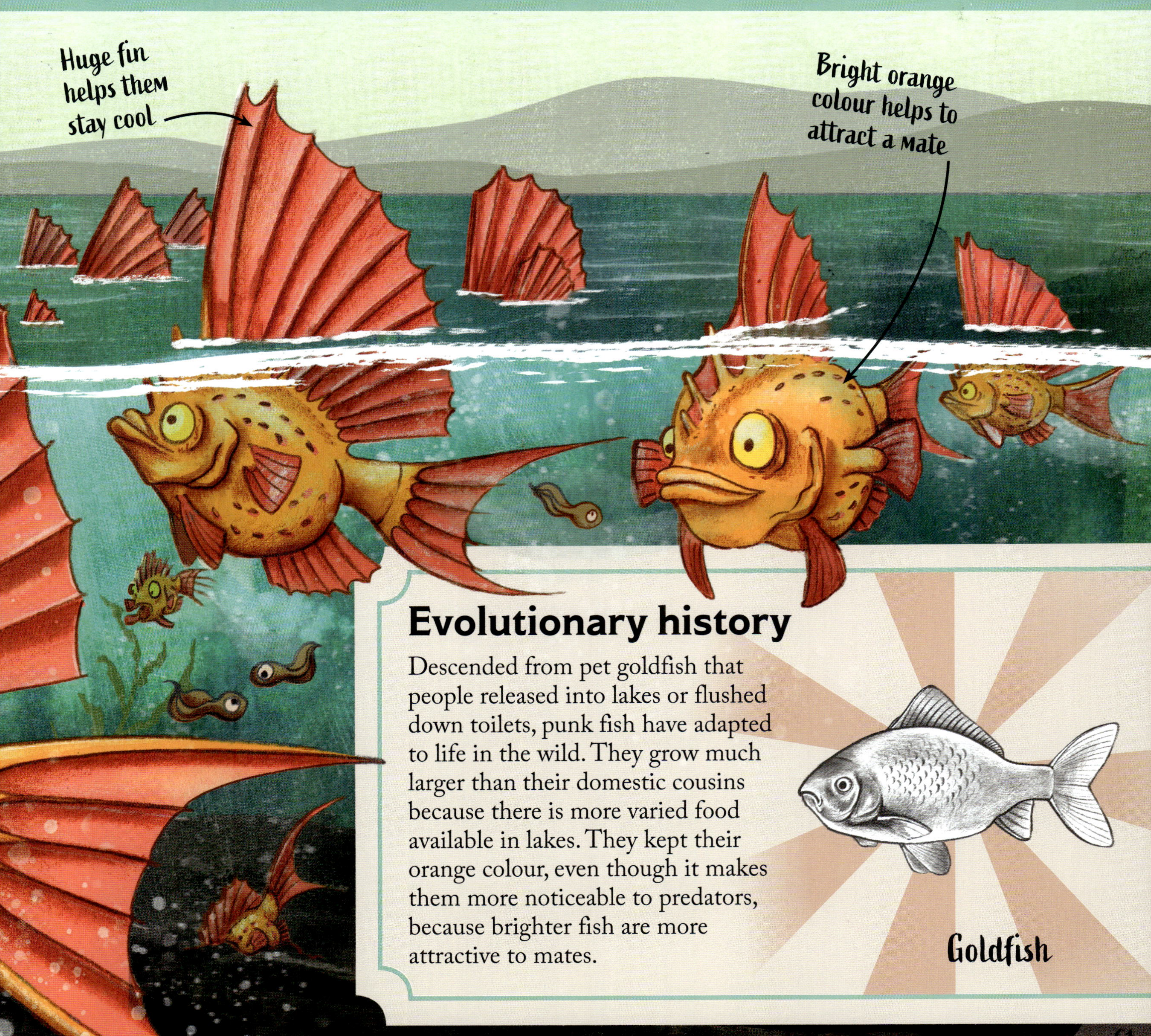

Evolutionary history

Descended from pet goldfish that people released into lakes or flushed down toilets, punk fish have adapted to life in the wild. They grow much larger than their domestic cousins because there is more varied food available in lakes. They kept their orange colour, even though it makes them more noticeable to predators, because brighter fish are more attractive to mates.

GAPING DEATH FISH
Melanocetus insidiosus

These strange, flat fish are masters of disguise, changing colour to blend in with the sea-floor. Males are a hundred times smaller than females and have no teeth to feed, so they live for just a few days. Their only aim is to find a mate before they die. Females are well-camouflaged, so males rely on scent to track them down. They must approach with caution though, as females often mistake a potential mate for food and gobble them up!

Diet

Gaping death fish have a flat, green spine sticking out of their nose, which looks like seaweed. As it waves gently in the water, it attracts hungry fish and sea slugs, which get a nasty surprise when they try to take a bite. The gaping death fish opens its enormous mouth and swallows them whole!

Habitat

Found throughout the Atlantic Ocean, gaping death fish are most common in cooler waters away from the equator. That's because they are descended from deep-sea fish that adapted to lower temperatures. By day, they rest on the sea-floor, waiting for prey to come to them. At night, they bury themselves in the sand to hide from predators.

Evolutionary history

Climate change reduced the amount of oxygen in the ocean, driving many deep-sea fish extinct. To survive, humpback anglerfish moved closer to the surface where they adapted to life in the shallows. More light reaches the sea-floor here, so their famous glowing lure no longer stood out, making it useless for attracting prey. Instead, they evolved to produce light in their skin, which they use for camouflage, and their lure evolved to look more like seaweed, to attract prey in the shallows.

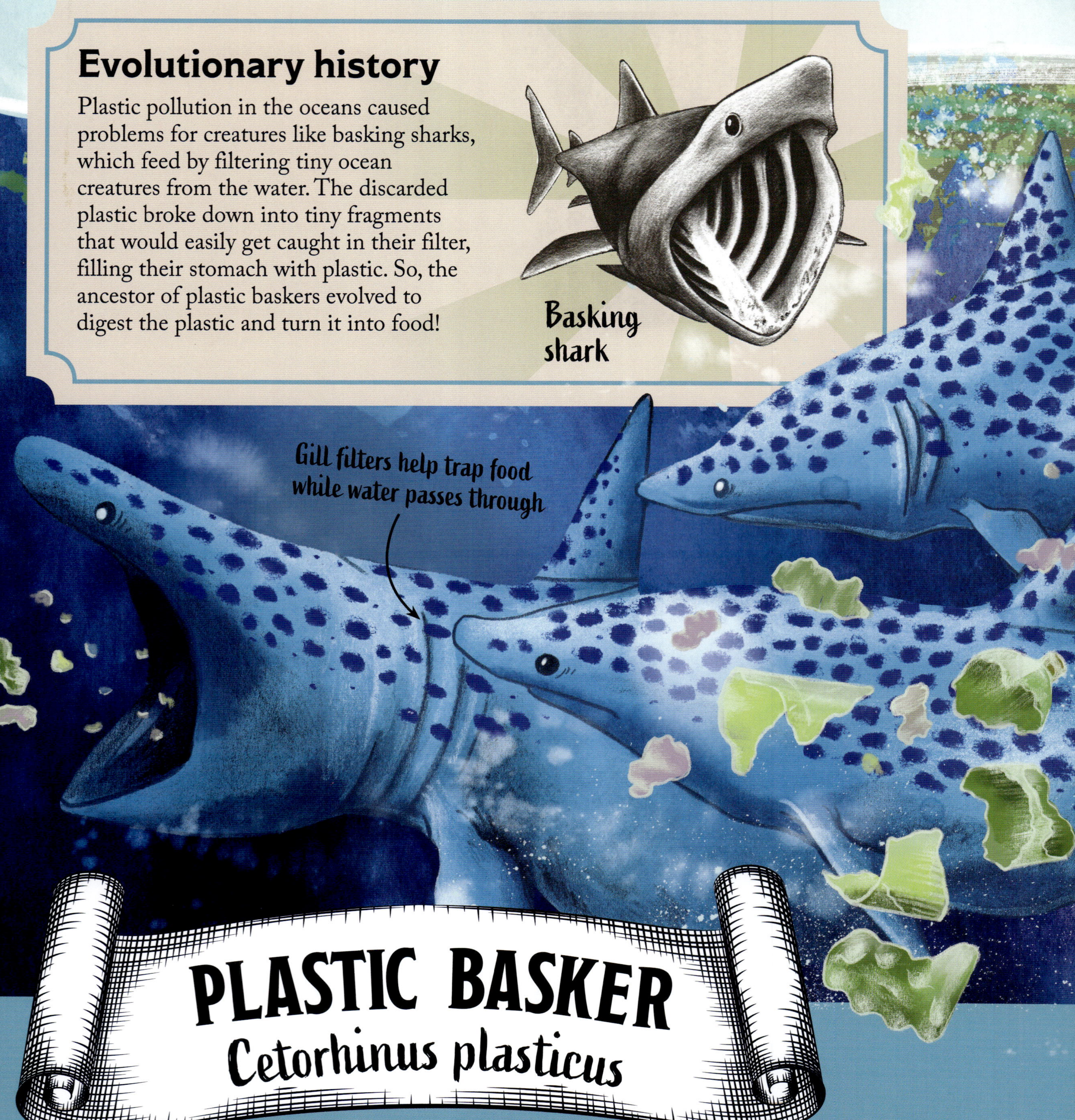

PLASTIC BASKER

Cetorhinus plasticus

These gentle giants are the ocean's cleaners. By feeding on plastic that humans polluted the waters with, they have improved the environment for other creatures. Plastic is a plentiful food source, allowing them to grow even larger than their ancestors. Their huge size means they have no major predators, so they don't need camouflage. Their brilliant blue skin and purple spots help them to attract a mate.

Diet

With their mouths wide open, plastic baskers swim through the water, trapping zooplankton and plastic fragments in special filters in their gills, while letting the water pass through. Plastic often contains lots of harmful chemicals, so they evolved an enlarged liver to break down these toxins and release them in their pee. That's what gives them their large belly!

Habitat

Found throughout the Pacific Ocean, plastic baskers spend the summer in cooler climates and migrate to tropical waters in the winter. On their long journey, they visit places where ocean currents cause plastic waste to build up, such as the Great Pacific Garbage Patch between Hawaii and California. Hundreds of plastic baskers gather here each spring to feast and breed.

SMARTY FIN
Gadus piscatus

Smarty fins are very intelligent fish, making use of objects in their environment as tools to help them hunt more efficiently. Their favourite trick is to use plastic fishing nets that were discarded by humans to catch other fish. Older smarty fins in the shoal teach this method to younger fish, passing it down from generation to generation.

Diet

When the shoal finds an abandoned fishing net, each fish grabs a corner and they swim in opposite directions. With the net stretched between them, they wait for smaller fish to get caught. They use the long, fleshy whisker on their chin to sense prey struggling in the net, even in murky water. When they've eaten their fill, these nomadic fish discard the net so that they can swim freely – they'll find another one easily enough!

Habitat

These intelligent and adaptable fish are found in coastal waters around Greenland, Iceland and Norway. They tend to spend their days in the depths and move closer to the ocean surface at night. Their large fins help them stay cool in the future's warmer ocean waters.

The theory

Driven by the need to find food and protect themselves, some animals have evolved the intelligence needed to master tool use. Over time, individuals that use tools are more likely to survive and pass this trait on to their offspring, ensuring that the next generation become smarter, more skilled tool-users.

Evolutionary history

Overfishing and climate change had a devastating effect on ocean creatures, so predatory fish like the Atlantic cod had to work harder to find prey. Humans had littered the oceans with plastic fishing nets, which weren't biodegradable, so they were still there long after humans went extinct. The smartest cod figured out how to turn this trash into a useful tool.

Atlantic cod

Hook-shaped lip to pick up fishing nets

Fleshy whisker to detect prey

Desert hound

Trash mole

Dear Reader,

Thank you for taking the time to read my book – many years of work has gone into studying these incredible creatures and developing my theories about how they evolved. The remarkable animals that I've described in this book are just a small selection of the many unique beings I encountered on my epic journey into the future. I hope one day I will get a chance to tell you more.

Many of the species I discovered in the future had been shaped by the legacy that humans left behind. From the trash moles that evolved to feed on our waste, to the cement snails that took up residence in our abandoned buildings, humans left an enduring mark on planet Earth, which animals had to adapt to. But my journey also reminded me that nature is resilient. Evolution ensures that animals can adapt and thrive in almost any situation, provided they have enough time.

Although life on Earth is resilient, not all species survived to be part of that future world. There were many extinctions. Some creatures simply couldn't adapt fast enough to keep up with the huge changes to the environment that humans had brought about.

After you have finished reading this book, I hope you will take some time to ponder how humans can have a more positive impact on the planet. The world is a big and complicated place, but we can all make choices that help the natural world. From planting wildflowers in your garden and only buying things you really need to encouraging your local government representatives to support environmental policies, there are many actions we can take that will help make the world a better place for wildlife and for humans.

Right now, many species are facing extinction because of humans. If we want to help the amazing, curious and remarkable creatures living on Earth today, we must do what we can to reduce our negative impact on the natural world. The species that survive today will become the ancestors to endless more beautiful and wonderful species many millions of years from now.

The future is not set in stone. The fantastical creatures in this book may never come to exist, but other even more incredible animals may arise, if we give nature a chance to thrive.

Yours sincerely,

Beatrice Russel

Professor Beatrice Russel
Time Walker

Feathered flower

GLOSSARY

adaptation a characteristic that helps an animal to survive and reproduce

ancestor an earlier species that evolved into the species being described

aquatic a species that spends most or all of its time in water

camouflage a colour or pattern that helps an animal blend in with its surroundings

canine long, pointed teeth that are found on either side of the front teeth

carnivore a species that mainly eats meat

climate the long-term average weather pattern of a region, such as temperature and rainfall

climate change long-term changes to the average weather patterns on Earth

descendant a later species that evolved from the species being described

diet the types of food that an animal eats

ecosystem a community of species that interact with each other and with the non-living parts (such as water, air and rocks) of their environment

ectothermic a species that controls its body temperature using the environment (cold-blooded)

endothermic a species that generates its own body heat from within (warm-blooded)

habitat the type of environment that a creature usually lives in

herbivore a species that mainly eats plants

incubator an object that provides the ideal conditions (such as warmth) for an egg to develop

larva young form of some animals (e.g. insects or frogs) that hatch from eggs and look different from the adult

nocturnal a species that is mostly active at night

omnivore a species that regularly eats both plants and meat

pesticide a substance that is used to kill pests, such as insects or fungi

pollinate the transfer of pollen from one flower to another, which leads to the production of seeds

pollution the release of harmful substances into the environment

predator an animal that hunts and kills other animals to eat

scavenger an animal that eats food that other animals have discarded

stamen the male reproductive organ of a plant, where the pollen develops

UV light a type of light with a very short wavelength, which some animals can see, but humans can't

This book was born out of my fascination with evolution and the natural world. Although a lot of imagination has gone into each chapter, everything you have read is rooted in real science!

To imagine the future animals that might one day evolve, I spoke to many expert scientists, used my own scientific knowledge as an evolutionary biologist and did lots of research. Although the exact details are extremely difficult to predict, it is very likely that the creatures of the future will have evolved based on the scientific principles described in this book, such as symbiosis, convergent evolution, attracting a mate and most importantly – natural selection!

I hope that reading this book will spark your own imagination and that you'll take a moment to wonder about all the incredible creatures that might evolve one day. I'd also encourage you to look at the amazing plants and animals around you and consider why they have evolved to look, think and act the way that they do. It's this curiosity about the natural world that drives us to learn more about it and to care for it and protect it as best we can. I hope you never lose that magical curiosity – I never lost mine!

Claire Asher, PhD

ACKNOWLEDGEMENTS

I am extremely grateful to the many scientists who generously gave up their time to help me ensure that the content of this book is rooted in science. In particular, I'd like to thank Jack Ashby, Mairin Balisi, Phil Barden, Sahas Barve, Erica McAlister, Alexis M. Mychajliw, Sharlene E. Santana and Andrew Swafford for providing their invaluable insights and inspiration during initial brainstorming sessions, which helped me to develop ideas for the animals featured in this book.

I am also very thankful for the constructive feedback I received from Jack Ashby, Mairin Balisi, Phil Barden, Nicolas Hubert, Jonathan Losos, Jingmai O'Connor and Alexus Roberts Hugghis on early versions of the text, which helped me to refine the book to make it as realistic and scientifically rigorous as possible. I'd also like to thank my partner Dan for providing a sounding board for my ideas and helping me make sure that the creatures in this book are not just scientifically realistic, but also fun and interesting.

I would like to say a huge thank you to the incredibly talented Fiona Fogg, whose beautiful illustrations have brought my ideas to life, and to Emma Hobson for all her hard work on the design and layout of the book. Finally, this book would not have been possible without the tireless help, patience and creative input from my editor at Bloomsbury Publishing, Emily Ball, to whom I am very grateful.

Claire Asher, PhD